Feeling
For
Eggs

Feeling For Eggs

Elizabeth Patton

Clare Songbirds
Publishing House

Clare Songbirds Publishing House
ISBN 978-1-957221-08-3
Feeling for Eggs © 2023 Elizabeth Patton

Printed in the United States of America
FIRST EDITION

Clare Songbirds Publishing House
140 Cottage Street
Auburn, New York 13021
www.claresongbirdspub.com

Contents

Acknowledgements

The author wishes to thank the following publishers who previously published stories in this collection.

"Feeling for Eggs," published in *Confessions: Fact of Fiction, A Collection of Short Stories and Memoir*, Herta B. Feely & Marian O'Shea Wernicke, editors (Chrysalis Editorial, 2010)

"Waiting for a Sign," *Peacock's Feet*

Foreward

By Rachael Ikins, student of Elizabeth Patton, author of *Eating the Sun*, *Just Two Girls*, *For Kate*, *Totems*, and *A Piglet for David*

Elizabeth Patton's crisp prose and dry humor invite the reader into a cross-section of a time in history and the women who journey through it. The author explores everything from race relations in the 30s and 40s in the South as the character of a five-year-old child cries when the black woman who cooks and cleans their house and who is the adult with whom the child spends most of her time, walks home every night. "Why can't I go with her?"

Full of textured mother/daughter relationships, the reader sees generations of women pass down dysfunction and disappointment, no matter how much a young woman achieves. Society limited women to kitchen and home in the 50s. Patton's characters are no exception. Not surprisingly their frustration wreaks itself in subtle ways on their own daughters.

Patton's ladies, like characters in British literature who drink tea for all occasions, like to serve a beverage at any crisis be it an unwanted pregnancy, death, or a daughter's visit home with her lesbian lover. While many glasses of lemonade or sweet tea are swallowed, these women enjoy their Scotch and gin just as much.

Throughout the collection Patton has smartly placed a particular character, Luttrell, so we can follow her journey. Patton shows us that in small town Southern culture, fascination with who is related to whom is as important a pastime as it is for the Scots in Diana Gabaldon's *Outlander* novels.

Conveying a slight ambiance of darkness and angst reminiscent of Faulkner and Flannery O'Conner, Patton introduces us to a lesbian couple— "Boston marriage," college English professors, schoolteachers, poets and artists, and their mamas, grandmothers, and maiden aunts.

This feminist collection is filled with survivors. The author brings us to present day where, in one story, an older woman has moved to a condo in Florida where residents are not allowed to bring lawn chairs to sit on the grass. The author conveys aging as characters who used to till a whole vegetable garden grow only a couple of pots of tomatoes and cucumbers, restricted to that condo balcony.

Many of the stories conclude with delightful surprise endings. In others, the vividness of detail lets the actual faces of those women float into your consciousness, as if this is someone you know.

From the start you imagine yourself that small girl kneeling with eyes squeezed shut, forced to extend her tender hand under the house's darkness for any eggs that fell through, by her mother, while not knowing if a monster is going to bite that hand. Only that she will get spanked for lying if she leaves any wasted eggs.

You realize when you turn the final page, that the title, *Feeling for Eggs* aptly describes the secret lives of families. You realize a secret can be as fragile as a child's hand or an eggshell. Shattering it might reveal much more than you bargained for.

Feeling for Eggs

When I think about my earliest memory, it is always summer, and I am wandering in the yard around the farmhouse. My mother would put me out after breakfast and hook the screen door. I had time and. space, but I had to share it with a white leghorn rooster, whose main concern was guarding his property and treating me as a stranger. Once he saw me, he ran toward me, and I ran toward the lot fence. He would spur me if I didn't make it.

One morning he came toward me, and I began running and screaming. My mother ran from the house, yelling at the rooster, but she was also yelling at me. "Stop! Stop! He won't hurt you now." But I wouldn't stop until I made the fence. She pulled me off the boards and ran with me over to the chicken coop. "You stay in here until I come for you." She slid the latch, and I began crying and shaking the door. Nothing gave, and I began to investigate the cracks in the walls.

I heard her screaming, "Get away. Go home. I'll get the sheriff to you." Through a crack I could see that she was standing at the top of the hill, looking down the path through the pecan trees. There was someone coming up fast through the trees. He kept coming, and she kept yelling. "Get away from here. I don't want you here."

He gave her a wild look and climbed up on the well frame. He unhooked the bucket and threw it in. Then he began a descent into the water. As he went down, he yelled. She stopped yelling and ran into the house. He kept yelling like nothing I had heard before, long wails that had no end.

When she came back, she stood on the porch, her hands around her elbows, and she was quiet. For a long time there were no sounds but the moaning of the man and the clucking of the chickens around the coop.

I sat down and waited. I wandered around the hen nests. One hen was on the nest. "Good chickie," I said and patted her red feathers. There were some eggs in the nests. I found the basket and began to gather them.

I liked this part of chicken raising. What I didn't like was going under our house to find eggs that the hens dropped. The house was low on rocks in the back and open. I could barely get under to look for eggs. My mother would send me under, and I would fight her. It's dark under there. I don't want to go."

"You'll go. We need those eggs."

Then I would hit her legs, and she would pick me up and shove me under. It was so dark that I would pull myself along with my right hand feeling in front of me. I was so afraid of what might be around me. When I did find an egg, I put it in a pan and dragged it along. "And don't break any." That was the refrain in my mind. Frightened of the dark and the unknown, I could feel my heart. Sometimes there were little noises I didn't want to hear, and my heart beat wildly. Maybe I would find one or two eggs. Those I left would remain secrets.

In the coop I put the basket by the door and sat down on a feed bag. I must have fallen asleep. Sometime later my mother picked me up and took me to the house.

"Where is he?" I asked.

"Who?"

I looked at her and wondered what she had done. Was the man still in the well? I looked at the well and then back at her.

"The man in the well."

"Now, Audrey, there's no man in the well. You had a bad dream. I've told you about going to the coop and staying."

"I got the eggs for you, Mother."

"Thank you, baby. You're a good girl."

I nestled against her, and we went over to the glider and sat for a while. I never saw the man again. I asked my father about the man in the well, and he told me I must have made him up.

"You know how you make up things, Audrey." I never wanted to go near the well. When I had to, I watched carefully and listened.

Sometime after that day a car came to our house, and my mother left with two men. One was my Uncle Sterling and the other one I didn't know. My father knew him though.

I stayed out in the yard and watched them drive down the hill. Then I wandered out to the washtubs under the big pecan. Asmolia had the fire burning around the big black pot.

"You going to stay with me all day?"

"I guess so. Daddy has gone to work."

"You're in the way now. You go over there and swing."

I went over and began swinging. After a while Asmolia's husband, Zark, came up. As my swing went their way, I could hear them talking.

"Did she do it?" He asked her. She was bent over the washboard, and I didn't hear what she said. She looked up toward me. "She's a pistol, ain't she?" I thought she was talking about me.

Zark shook his head and moved on to the field. She began pulling sheets out of the pot with a stick and dumping them into the tub. She checked the clothesline and pushed the poles higher before she went back to rinsing.

Then I thought that she was talking about my mother. A pistol, I didn't know about any pistol. Maybe she had killed the man in the well.

2

I kept swinging, my legs going higher and higher. Asmolia hung up the clothes. When she finished, she looked up at me. "Come on now, Audrey. Your mama said for me not to let you out of my sight.

"Not now, Asmolia. You stay here with me. I'll let the cat die in a minute."

"You hurry up now. I got to. Do the housework and cook dinner for your daddy. He's coming home today to check on you, and then he's going back to work."

"When's she coming back?"

"I don't know, Audrey. She said, 'Expect me when you see me.' That's all I know."

That night before I went to sleep, my mother came to my room. "I'm back, Audrey. I'll see you in the morning."

As I drifted off, I could them talking in the kitchen, but the words didn't make any sense.

"Did he give you any trouble?"

"He was all right, but he cried at the end."

"The surprise of it all, I guess. Did you have any trouble with the car?"

"No, Bruton's car is like ours, only a couple of years older."

"I always think that a Ford will stay with you. A good all-round car. "

"You want some more soup, Delbert?"

"No, Asmolia made me a big dinner. The best okra I've had all season."

"Was Audrey all right?"

"Just the same, hanging around Asmolia and in the way. You know how she is on Mondays. You'd think she never had any company."

Monday, washday, Asmolia, swinging, the fire around the pot, a visit from Zark, week after week, and the crying when Asmolia left. "Come back tomorrow," I would plead.

"Now you hush up. I'll be by one day before Monday. You a big girl now, too big to be crying when I leave."

The next morning, I asked about the car, but my mother just told me she had to take a trip.

"Was it a Ford?"

"I don't know, Audrey. I never notice cars."

The rooster continued to chase me, and I kept on gathering eggs. The rooster never relented and then began to attack my mother. Not long after one of his most vicious displays, we had chicken for Sunday dinner.

After we ate that day, we took a drive up the Sardis Road. Just across the branch from our house lived Aunt Edith and Uncle Utney. We never saw them except on their place. Sometimes he would sew on

3

a machine out in the yard, but I don't believe I ever saw him sew. I heard that he did. Maybe my mother told me.

"When did she leave?" my father asked.

"Maybe a month ago, I guess," she answered.

"What about Uncle Utney? Where is he?" I wanted to know.

"They both are gone," she answered.

The house had weeds in the yard, and kudzu was covering the barn. I looked hard in case one of them might appear and wave as they used to.

The next afternoon Uncle Sterling and Aunt Sukie came by in their buggy. They were on their way to town.

"Do you need anything?" he asked my mother.

"Can't think of anything."

"Uncle Utney and Aunt Edith have gone away," I said. "We went by there yesterday."

"Is she doing all right?" my mother asked.

"She's with her family over in Vidalia," Aunt Sukie said. "We haven't heard from Utney."

I looked at them carefully. There was something I couldn't understand. Why wouldn't they know about both of them? Did they take the sewing machine with them? I forgot to look. Maybe it was still in the weeds near the house.

Someone rented their farm after a while, and then we moved to town, our farm sold to some people across the river. Asmolia and Zark moved somewhere out of the county.

Aunt Edith and Uncle Utney drifted from my mind. We hardly ever saw Aunt Sukie and Uncle Sterling. I never knew who was related to whom until I was grown. I knew that they were my mother's relatives, but no one talked about them.

Years went by, and I came home from college for my mother's funeral. I never knew that she had cancer until my father called to tell me she had died. I took the bus home from the funeral, wondering why everything happened that way with my mother.

A very old couple came to the service and sat near my father and me. "Aunt Sukie and Uncle Sterling," he whispered.

As the service progressed, my mind began to spin around the days when we lived on the farm. I saw my mother in the yard with that white leghorn rooster. I saw her running toward the pecan orchard and heard her screaming at the man. The man in the well. Who was the man in the well? Where did Uncle Utney and Aunt Edith go?

The casket showed my mother as a pretty woman, a woman still young in her forties. I would think of her much later in my life as even younger and stronger.

After the cemetery service we drove back to the house. I asked my father about that day the man came running up to the house and got into the well.

"Uncle Utney had one of his fits, Audrey. Your mother was just trying to protect you."

"He was the man in the well?"

"That's what your mother said. Didn't you see him?"

"I guess so, but I was looking through cracks in the chicken coop."

He looked puzzled. He didn't seem to understand why I was in the chicken coop. "She said that you were playing in the yard when he came up."

"No, I'm sure of that. I was in the coop the whole time he was there."

A few people came back to the house, a few businesspeople my father knew and some of circle friends of my mother. "You poor girl without a mother," they said over and over.

I walked over to Aunt Sukie and Uncle Sterling, who were the only family there.

"What a pretty girl you turned out to be."

"Thank you. Aunt Sukie."

Uncle Sterling looked at me, trying to recognize the little girl in me. "Why, I remember you when that old white rooster used to run you down. He was a mean one. He got so mean that your mama had to kill him. I remember going by to see if she needed anything one day and that old rooster was slung over the clothesline. She had wrung his neck."

"I remember him all right. I was such a little girl that he knew he could hurt me."

I waited for them to say something about my mother, but they seemed interested in their food. I began to think about the man in the well again—Uncle Utney.

"You know, Uncle Sterling, you can clear up something about my mother. Remember that day that you came to our house with another man and took my mother away?"

Uncle Sterling looked at me carefully. "I'll never forget that day. You were just a little bit of a thing then. Asmolia was washing that day, and she took care of you." He looked across the room at my father and then back to me. "I guess you ought to know. Your mama never wanted you to know."

"Know what, Uncle Sterling?"

"That day we took Utney to Milledgeville. We told him we were taking him to Vidalia to visit his in-laws."

"Milledgeville?"

"Your mama and the sheriff and I took him. She drove and we sat in the back seat with him. He was right pleased to be going to Sid's

5

place. He always liked his wife's people, you know."

Aunt Sukie shook her head. "Poor old Utney. He was never crazy. He was just sick. I've said that to Sterling a thousand times. His own brother."

"Your mama should never have done that to him, and to think that I was part of it. The worst thing as I think back was Edith running after the car yelling, "What did he do? Why are you taking him away?" I looked back and saw her standing out in the road, her apron over her face."

My father came by and stopped. "Have some more food. You people getting caught up?"

"Audrey and I were just talking about the old days," Uncle Sterling said. Aunt Sukie just looked at her food.

My father passed to another group, and Uncle Sterling looked back at me. "The other picture that just won't leave my mind is when we got to the hospital. Utney knew that he wasn't in Vidalia right away. 'This isn't Vidalia. This isn't Sid's place,' he said. Your mother ran in for help while we held him in the backseat. I've thought of that day a lot over the years."

"I would think so. I would think so." I began to think about my mother and wondered how much strength she had needed to drive someone to the mental hospital. She would have been about my age, still young enough to be in college.

"You know, he died there, far away from his family," Aunt Sukie said.

I didn't know that he had died there. I assumed that he and his wife were in Vidalia. My mother must have known.

After people left, my father said that he was glad that I had seen Uncle Sterling and Aunt Sukie. "We didn't keep up with them for years and years. Your mother didn't get on with them. I'm surprised they came."

My father and I didn't say anything much about my mother. We had never talked about her. She always seemed to be around talking to us. We just let her talk, and now we didn't have the habit of talking.

As I took the bus back to school, I tried to think about that day when I saw the man in the well. I didn't ever think that he was Uncle Utney. I wondered if I could ever have talked with my mother about that day if I had wanted to.

I began to think that I had grown up. I had learned some family secrets my mother would have denied. Perhaps her funeral was the appropriate place to hear them, but I would never know.

As the years have gone by, there are times that I know that I can never forget that little girl, scared, groping in dark spaces, feeling for eggs.

Waiting for a Sign

I need to sleep. My doctor says that I need complete rest. He wants me to eat. I don't want to eat. I don't want to nourish this body any longer. When I change my gown, I look at myself in the mirror. There are scales on my arms. My long sleeves cover them, but I scratch them through the fabric. I am getting a hump on my back. I'm beginning to lose my breasts. I want to hide myself in bedclothes and never show myself to anyone. The doctor comes and tells me that I have to take responsibility for my disease.

"Now, Mrs. Larabee, there are all kinds of folks suffering from pellagra. They been eating too much corn and not enough stuff with vitamins. I know you've always kept a good table for your family and your friends. You've starved your body, and you must start to feed yourself. You will do that, won't you?"

I tell him I will, but I won't. The girls bring in food for me, and I nibble a little. They ask me what I want, and I say, "Just a cup of black coffee and a few soda crackers. That's about all I can manage."

Whatever I eat just goes through me, and I feel weak. I'm tired. Women get tired, but no one seems to bother. We get married young, have child after child, work in the fields, and keep the house, all the while worrying. Our husbands ask us what's wrong, and we say, "It's nothing" and go on with our business of living. We have our secrets that husbands and doctors will never know.

Mr. Larabee has too much on his mind to worry about me. Last year there was a terrible drought. "1932 we'll always remember, Maud," he said. "I just don't know how we'll ever make it."

It's bad enough for women to suffer, but we're used to it. Men just don't have the experience in suffering we do. There are things you can't help it seems like. You have to trust in God to know what you can take and what you can't. God knows we're strong people, I reckon. I want to be, and I know Mr. Larabee is.

When we married, he was free and clear. He didn't owe anybody. He never meant me to suffer. I remember his telling me that I would never have to go to the fields to work with him. After the war his mother went into the fields, and he never forgot the humiliation that he felt to see her working alongside his father. "Here was a woman who had tended a rose garden and painted watercolors and directed a house full of servants and been a mother and wife," he said, "and she became a

7

worn-out field hand, dying of overwork." He promised me that I would not let me go that way, and he meant it. I see hurt in his eyes now when he knows that he let me down. Life has worked out differently from what I thought.

There's a picture of me over there on the dresser. I was eighteen then, and I was wearing a big hat with feathers. Mr. Larabee says I was the prettiest girl in Burke County, and that's why he waited for me to grow up. I always looked up to him. He's ten years older than I. He's strong and he's good. He never meant me to suffer.

Every time I had a child, he made sure I got the doctor. Some folks just have the grannies come over, but he never wanted them. Why, there are women I know of who do the birthing themselves, just asking their husbands to hand them things. When I started yelling loud, the doctor always gave me something to make it easier. Each one of the five children was a hard one to birth. Mr. Larabee was always careful about me. He brought in a woman afterwards to help me, usually Aunt Sadie, who lives on the place.

Until this trouble with Mary Sue, I thought we could get along all right. Mary Sue was a smart one. I meant her to go on to school in town and take that teachers' course at Statesboro. I sold vegetables and eggs to get a little extra, and she was working her way, too. She was the oldest, and when she got in trouble, she came to me. She couldn't let her father know. I gave her some money I had hidden in the mattress when I got married. My daddy gave me fifty dollars private-like before I left home. "You may have need of this, Maud, so keep it to yourself." I told Mary Sue to take it and find someone to help her get rid of the baby. She died, and Mr. Larabee knows everything now except where she got the money.

I can never tell him. He's a good man, and I don't want to add to his sorrow. The sin is mine, and I will suffer for it. I seem to think about Mary Sue all the time. Sometimes at night I come awake, thinking that she's in the room. "Mary Sue, Mary Sue, where are you?" I listen, hoping that she'll come into the room the way she used to when I called her. Yesterday Mr. Larabee and Joe and Sally and Reba went to the funeral at Habersham.

They left the knee baby with Aunt Sadie. Mr. Larabee's people helped start the church, and we used to go every Sunday. Mr. Larabee and the children still go, but I haven't felt up to going anywhere in such a long time.

The three children work on the place with their father. He never wanted the girls to work, but I told him that we couldn't be proud any longer. Before the last child, I used to go out and help them sometimes, too. Mr. Larabee never liked it, but he got used to it. Joe went to eighth grade and stopped off. He wants to get his own land in a few years.

He's a worker, and his father admires him. The girls still go to school, and we encourage them to do their best.

Mr. Larabee never says so, but I know I'm a burden to him. For about six months I've been up and down ever since I had this last one. I thought nature had left me, but instead I was carrying another one. And me over forty, too.

I worry that Oliver is not right. He doesn't cry much, and folks say that he's smart that way. His eyes bother me. They look dead. I think he's slow. They always say if your baby's not right the mother has mocked some poor afflicted person. I can't think of anyone I talked about but remember thinking about whether I could take care of a baby palsied like my sister, Pauline. She came too late when my mother was too old. Mr. Larabee worries, too. He tries to cheer me up. "It's God's way to keep us humble and make us strong," he says.

Ever since the baby came, I've been in this room by myself. Mr. Larabee has a room on the other side of the house. The doctor told him to leave me to myself. The girls keep the room clean, and I feel like a visitor in my own house. They move me into the kitchen for a little while, and they scrub the floor. The room smells like Octagon soap. It seems like I can smell more than I used to. The cooking odors are stronger than they were, and I wish I could eat but I can't. Mr. Larabee fixed the screen in this room and bought new mosquito netting for the bed. At night I hear the mosquitoes singing around me. I sometimes feel that I'm spinning, and the mosquitoes are getting louder and louder. When I can't sleep at night, I look through the window into the backyard.

For several nights now I have seen a man standing by the gate. When I look in the morning, I just see a tree where he was standing. During the day I wonder if he'll come back. I think that he's waiting for me to come out to him.

He reminds me of a poem that I learned a long time ago. I don't know why I remember it, but I want to be able to say it again. When I was young, my mama used to say, "Why, Maud can read and recite like nobody's business." At the eighth-grade graduation I did some selections from "Maud" by Alfred Lord Tennyson. Miss Dawson, my teacher, said, "That will be real sweet for you to do 'Maud,' your being named Maud and loving flowers so." I worked hard on it, and everyone said I did well at the program. The graduation part was in the morning, and then we had a big dinner on the ground. My mama filled up a trunk with food, putting her special lemon pies in the tray on top. Everybody always said that her lemon pies were the best anywhere. I never learned to make them well. That day my Daddy got an attack of appendicitis, and a doctor from Augusta came down by train and operated on him in our kitchen. I remember how scared I was that something should happen to him and that we'd be left by ourselves. I haven't thought about that day in a long time. It's funny how one little thing can make you think of a lot of things. I like the part of the poem that starts, "Come into the garden, Maud." I'm going to try to remember the words and say them for Reba. She came into my room last night and asked me if I wanted anything because she heard me talking. I told her I was trying to remember a poem.

Reba is only ten, but she loves words. She cuts out things from *The Christian Herald* and puts them in a keepsake book. Mr. Larabee bought her a Bluehorse notebook special. He goes to town on Saturdays and buys what we need. When he came home in the buggy that day, Reba was waiting for him down at the gate. She ran with the notebook and showed me.

"I'm so happy, Mama. Now I'll have a book of my own."

Reba writes her own poems, but she doesn't show them to me. I hope I can remember the poem for her. She would like to read Tennyson's poetry. I wonder whatever happened to that book mama had. When she died, a lot of things were thrown out because no one seemed to want them. I should have spoken up for some books. I didn't have any place to put books then, and I never had time for reading. Sometimes when I'm out by the barn, I look in at the piano. We said we'd store the piano because no one in the family had room for it. It came from Philadelphia for my mother to play. Now the rats have it. I don't like to think what she would say. Sometimes I think we're losing ourselves in droughts and boll weevils and hard times. The harder we work the more we forget our people and their lives. I wonder what the end will be.

Last night I heard a baby cry and I wondered who had a baby at our house. I thought maybe Mary Sue was visiting with her baby. I started crying, "Mary Sue, bring in the baby." I came to, with Sally shaking me. "Wake up, Mama. It's just Oliver crying. It's not Mary Sue." In the half-light Sally looked like Mary Sue, her red braids loose and covering her shoulders. Mr. Larabee came in and sat with me. When he was sitting in the chair, I couldn't see the man in the garden, and I thought he might be gone. I asked Mr. Larabee if he saw the man in the garden.

"There's no man in the garden, Maud. You're just imagining. Hush up now. It's all right. See can you get back to sleep."

When I woke up later, he was gone. I eased out of bed and went to the window to see if the man was there. He was there waiting for me. I went to bed and began to say the poem until I couldn't remember anymore and then I fell asleep.

This morning Reba has a tray for me. She helps me up. "I'm going to give you a bath this morning, but first I brought some coffee for you."

"What time is it, Reba?"

"About five thirty. Poppa and Joe have been at the gin all night, but they'll take turns eating and then go back. Sally is going to help them, and I'm going to stay with you and Oliver." Reba has that same bright red hair from the Prescott side. She looks very serious and younger than her ten years.

"Thank you, Reba." I take the coffee. "You're treating me fancy this morning with the gold-band cup." My mama gave me these dishes when I was married, and we use them for company. Every day we use the ironstone.

"You're special, Mama."

"I don't feel special, I'm afraid."

"What can I get you to eat? I can make eggs and bacon."

"I'll try some toast, Reba."

"What about some of that blackberry jam, too?"

"I'll try some and a little bacon. I can't disappoint the cook, can I?"

She smiles and kisses me. I drink the coffee. By the time Mr. Larabee comes, I am eating the toast. He is tired and trying not to let on. Ginning time always takes it out of him.

"Maud, how are you?"

"Maybe a little better this morning. Reba really coaxed me into eating. She's a good girl."

"I want you to eat like the doctor told you. You can't leave us. I don't know what I'd do with two young girls and a baby. Sally wants to go to high school next year. I guess we can send her. I'm going to try."

"Thank you, Mr. Larabee." I don't want to ask about the funeral. I wait for him to speak.

"Brother Holland preached a good funeral sermon. He said that the Lord giveth and the Lord taketh away, but He always gives again. We have to know that and believe. 'Abide with Me' was the hymn at the end. A lot of us were crying through the last stanza. I kept thinking about Mary Sue and how she was wanting something special beyond this place. I kind of think we owe it to her to keep trying. I can't always see the end of it sometimes, but I know you mean well with the children. You've always been a good mother."

I begin to cry and wipe my tears on the sheet. "I'll try to get well, Mr. Larabee. You go get your breakfast now. I'll see you at dinner. Maybe I'll try to get up a little today."

Reba comes in as he leaves. "I brought the water for your bath, Mama. Let's start."

"Fine, Reba."

"You know, Mama, I've been thinking that I'd like to be a teacher the way Mary Sue wanted. I like to memorize poems and write little pieces. I know I could do good work.

"Mrs. Foster says I'm the best writer in the whole school."

"We're real proud of you, Reba."

11

"Mama, could you say some of the poem you were saying the other night?"

"I'll do a little. It's easy to learn. 'Come into the garden, Maud, for the black bat, Night, has flown, Come into the garden, Maud, I am here at the gate alone...' I'll tell you something if you promise not to tell."

"Sure, Mama."

"You see that tree out there in the yard? At night I've been thinking there was a man standing out there waiting for me. It's only the tree trunk."

Reba goes over to the window. "I can see why you thought it was a man. That's like making poetry, Mama."

"Would you let me read some of your poems sometime, Reba?"

"Would you really? Maybe tomorrow. I want to copy them out again. When she leaves, I hear her tell Mr. Larabee that I will get well. She knows I will.

In Front of the Camera

When the lights came on in the picture show, Claire had learned to sit and wait for her mother to take out her compact, powder her face, and put on lipstick. She and her mother had driven to Charleston as they usually did on Wednesdays to see a picture. As she watched the mostly female audience slowly file toward the exits, Claire thought about a line from the movie—"a woman is only beautiful when she is loved"—and she wanted to write it down in her scrapbook and paste some movie star pictures around it. It was the kind of extra touch that would impress her best friends, Jenny and Amelia.

"Come on, Claire. Let's go." Her mother took Claire's hand and led her to the door. The bright afternoon sun hurt Claire's eyes, and her yellow pinafore stuck to her back after sitting so long in the theater seat.

They headed toward their car, moving along crowded sidewalks, jostling against groups of sailors going in and out of bars and restaurants. The sailors often walked abreast down the sidewalks, pushing passersby to the curb. Claire held tightly to her mother's hand, afraid that she might somehow become separated from her. The sailors looked them over and sometimes made comments like "Hubba, hubba," and "Lady, leave your little girl home." Music spilled out into the street, and some of the sailors were singing "Pistol-packing Mama" as they moved along the sidewalk. Another group with young girls tight against their uniforms were swaying outside a doorway to the strains of "Goodnight, Irene." The walk to the car took so long, Claire thought, and she wondered why her mother couldn't find a place closer to the picture show to park the car.

As they drove home, Claire looked over at her mother and knew that she was in a good mood. She was always in a good mood when they went to Charleston.

"When is grandmother coming tomorrow, Mama?"

"In the afternoon, probably around four. Miss Dot Wheeler is driving her down from Spartanburg. I'll be up from my nap by then. Charlie Mae will leave us a cold supper. Do you want to invite Jenny or Amelia over to eat in the arbor with you?"

"Oh, could I, Mama?"

"Sure, that way I can talk more with grandmother."

Claire had never liked her grandmother. First of all, she talked all the time, and she'd say anything about you with you standing right there. Claire never forgot the time she told a whole room full of people about her mother's delivery. "My Lutrell was in labor for sixteen terrible hours, and finally this awful-looking little creature appeared, all wrinkled and long." Everyone then looked at Claire to see if she were still wrinkled and long. Claire didn't have to worry very much about her grandmother because gas rationing kept her visits infrequent.

When they came home that afternoon, Claire ran into the kitchen, hoping that Charlie Mae might still be working. She wanted to tell her about Mr. Skeffington. Telling Charlie Mae about the movies had become a ritual for Claire. She was disappointed to find the kitchen empty.

Charlie Mae had worked for Claire's grandmother and her mother, and the Queen Anne house with its various porches, turrets, and bay windows seemed to belong more to the woman who walked to work from a four-room house on the edge of town than it did to the inhabitants. Often Claire saw Charlie Mae more during the day than she did her mother, who usually woke up late and did little work around the house.

At 7:30am anyone nearby on Cleveland Avenue going out on the porch to pick up the paper and the milk might see a tall, straight black woman going down the driveway to the back door of the Godwin house. If it were summer, she carried a black umbrella and a grocery bag, often filled with vegetables from her small garden. Claire often sat on the back porch waiting for her.

"When did Charlie Mae leave, Mama?"

"Oh, she left early today. She had a funeral, and she had to dress in the white uniform and be one of the funeral officials."

When Claire's grandfather died three years ago, Claire had talked about him with Charlie Mae and asked her about funerals. Charlie Mae had told her about her special role as a church sister. Claire went to her mother and told her that Charlie Mae had to wear her uniform and sit with Claire at the funeral. "She knows more about funerals than we do," she told Lutrell. At the funeral Charlie Mae wore her uniform and sat with her arm around Claire in the front pew.

"I wanted to tell her about the movie."

"You can tell her in the morning, Claire. It's so hot in here. Let's go on the porch and have some lemonade. I think there's a pitcher in the refrigerator."

Claire put glasses on a tray and found the lemonade. She followed her mother up the long dark hall to the porch. She set down the tray, and her mother served the lemonade. They sat in the wicker chairs and looked out on the street. Claire looked back at her mother, who had slipped off her blue and white spectacles and curled her legs up in the chair. Claire thought that she looked like a movie star. Sometimes when Claire brushed her mother's hair or made up her face, she would ask Claire if she really looked like Janet Gaynor.

"Of course, you do, Mama. Daddy says so and everybody else,

too," and her mother would smile.

On Fridays Claire went with her to the beauty shop. Ida Jean would fix her mother's hair, turn around the chair, and ask Claire, "Now ain't your mama pretty?"

"Oh, yes," Claire would answer. Her mother had a wide forehead and tiny shaped eyebrows and blue eyes. She used blue eye eyeshadow. Her lips were a cupid's bow. Her fine blonde hair waved around her face. "Is that your mother?" someone once asked Claire, emphasizing the word mother. "She looks more like a sister."

When she went with her mother to the beauty shop, she always hoped that the conversation would be about her mother or about town gossip. She hated it when they talked about her. She had dark hair and dark eyes. "She's like the Godwins," they said. The Godwins were dark -skinned and dark-haired and dark-eyed, and they were tall and straight like the Indians in Wyeth illustrations. Ida Jean was related to Claire's mother, a cousin twice removed. Claire didn't know what that meant except that Ida Jean never came to visit them, but she knew all the family gossip.

"You know, Lutrell, Claire is looking more like the Godwins every day. I can see it in her eyes and her forehead. The Godwins always have those little squinty eyes that close up when they laugh."

They would look at Claire and laugh. Claire tried not to laugh and close her eyes.

"I know it, Ida Jean. I was so hoping she'd look like our people, but it's the chance you take when you marry into an ugly family."

"I never meant nothing about Tom Ray, who is as fine as they come. By the way, what do you hear from him?"

"Not a lot, but you know he's in the Pacific. Every time I go to the picture show, I just hope I see something about the Gilberts and the Marianas and all those little islands. I feel real proud when the *Movie Tone News* shows our boys in the Pacific."

"He's a real hero, Lutrell, an officer, too. We're all real proud of him."

Claire and her mother would walk home, both of them feeling good about themselves. Going to the beauty shop and going to Charleston were what Lutrell called "our little extravagances."

As they passed the dime store, Lutrell frequently asked Claire if she wanted to look at paper dolls. "We have time, Claire. Maybe they have some new movie stars you haven't seen."

"You know I've outgrown paper dolls, Mama." Claire looked hard at her mother. There was no way that Claire was going to fall for her mother's entreaties. She remembered playing with her Greer Garson dolls on the living room floor and leaving them time after time for her mother to pick up. One day Lutrell said, "The next time you leave your paper dolls on the floor, I'm going to burn them. You've got to learn to do what you're told." Claire left the paper dolls again, and her mother called her from her room and waited with a match in her hand. "Here, Claire, strike the match and light the paper. You brought it on yourself."

Claire looked at the paper dolls and the clothes piled in the grate. She was not going to let her mother know how much it hurt. She took the match, struck it against the box, and lit the paper. She watched the colors curl into each other. "Mama, you're mean, and I hate you." She didn't cry, but she had said something she had never said.

"Go to your room, Claire. What would your father say if he heard you?"

Your father had become such a technical term that Claire had no real feeling for the man behind it. Her mother never used it except to remind Claire that she had to appear at a final bar of justice. Sometimes Claire thought that if her father came back, her mother would meet him at the ship with a long list of infractions. "Now before you kiss me or say you're glad to be home, take a look at these awful things your daughter has done to worry and pester me."

When she watched her mother writing to him, she wondered what she said about her. Sometimes her mother read parts of the letters to Claire, who didn't recognize the life they lived. Her mother made up good stories. "He'll enjoy these letters," Lutrell said. "He needs cheering up."

While her mother was writing at the desk in the living room, Claire would wander over to the piano and pick out "We'll Meet Again" with one finger. Sometimes when she was in her room, she would just say the title of the song and think of her father. She went back in time. She was five years old, and he would call her when he came in from the hardware store. He would take her for a ride in her red wagon. Her favorite picture of the two of them showed her in the wagon, her father pulling it. She kept the snapshot on the wall over her desk in her room. Movie star pictures were taped around it.

As Claire and Lutrell sat on the porch, Mrs. Thomas, who lived next door, left her sprinkler for a few minutes and came over. Every afternoon she moved the sprinkler from one side of the yard to another, trying to save her lawn during the last days of August. "Well, did you two enjoy the movie?" she asked. They told her that they did. "One of these days I'll have to go in with you and see my grandchildren," she said.

"Just anytime," Lutrell responded. Mrs. Thomas wandered back over to her yard and began deadheading her roses.

"Are you going to ask Mrs. Thomas sometime, Mama"

"Of course not."

Claire had no response, and there was a short silence. Claire moved back to the movie. "That Bette Davis sure knows how to handle men, Mama. I could hardly look when she pushed Mr. Skeffington down those stairs." She looked toward the stairs in the hall. "Our stairs aren't tall enough for any pushing of wheelchairs."

Her mother laughed and poured them more lemonade. She leaned against the porch railing and looked toward the park. Sometimes she and Claire walked in the park and played a movie star game. Claire felt close to her mother when they could talk about movies. She would discuss the merits of each movie they saw. As her grandmother once remarked, "Now, Lutrell takes her pictures shows right seriously."

"Do you want to play movie star?" Claire asked.

Her mother turned around to face her. "Do you have any new ones I don't know?"

"I don't know, Mama. When I play movie star with Jenny and Amelia, I can always stump them, but you're too good."

"Here's one for you, Claire. Who is a male actor with the initials P. H.?"

"Oh, that's easy, Mama. Paul Henreid, who was in *Now, Voyager* with Bette Davis and Claude Rains." Claire had noticed that her mother's favorite male stars were blonde.

"That's very good, Claire." She smiled, humming a little and looking back toward the park. Twilight was settling in on the tall pines. "Did you have a good time today?"

"Sure, Mama. I liked the picture show. What I didn't like was having to walk so far from the car —all those sailors on the streets and that awful music played so loud."

"That was awful, wasn't it?"

Claire watched her mother closely. Somehow it didn't seem so awful for her mother. She thought about her mother and the sailors and put them into a movie. As they walked along, music started up and they began to dance. That's what happened in movies.

Her mother loved to dance, and she often turned on the radio in the living room and danced on the rug. Sometimes at night Claire could hear strains of "In the Mood" and "I'll Get By" and know that her mother had that dreamy look in her eyes as she glided across the floor. If she had trouble going to sleep, Claire would sneak down the stairwell to watch.

Sometimes at night Claire would close the door to her room and dance. Her favorite song that year was "People Will Say We're in Love." She would hum and dance around in her seersucker pajamas, pretending that she was Princess Elizabeth. Her mother had told her that the song was Elizabeth's favorite song now that she was in love with Prince Philip. When Claire went out, people said that she looked like the little princess, Margaret Rose. Claire was not impressed with either

17

one's looks, but she liked this comparison better than Ida Jean's. At least everyone didn't think she looked like an Indian. Lutrell took pains with Claire's hair, brushing and washing and curling until Claire wished she had no hair. She didn't look at all like the little princess, but her hair did. Her hair was thin and brown, and she had brown eyes. Her friends looked like Shirley Temple. Claire wanted ringlets or braids, one or the other but not little pin curls and a barrette.

After lunch the next day her mother took her usual afternoon nap. Charlie Mae was cleaning the kitchen when Claire wandered in.

"Have you seen my book?"

"What book, Claire?"

"Oh, you know, Charlie Mae. The one I've been reading to you."

Claire had made a habit of settling herself at the kitchen table and reading *Eight Cousins* to Charlie Mae while she washed the dishes or cooked. She had read the book several times, and each time she saw herself as Rose, a moral example to a group of older boy cousins. Claire wished that she had some older boy cousins. Her friend Amelia had a boy cousin who worked at the drugstore and gave them extra scoops of ice cream. Claire thought that Amelia was very lucky to have him, but she doubted that he ever asked Amelia for any advice about his life. The best part of the book Claire thought was the scene where Rose talks about smoking as a bad habit for her cousins. Charlie Mae agreed with Rose.

"It's a bad habit, all right. Your mama does not look ladylike smoking those cigarettes." Lutrell, at the end of a meal, would get another cup of coffee or another glass of iced tea and take out a pack of Chesterfields and smoke.

Claire nodded. "I've told her, too, but she doesn't listen."

"I'll bet she won't do any smoking while your grandmother is here." Charlie Mae chuckled. "Things pick up when your grandmother's around. It sure will seem like old times."

"I guess so." She found her book in a chair pushed under the table. "Here's my book, so I'll go out to the arbor to read."

She had called her friends about coming to supper, but they couldn't come. Betty Ann had invited Jenny and Amelia to go to the beach. There was no one else in third grade that she wanted to invite to have supper with her. Maybe she would eat by herself in the arbor and look at some movie magazines. Ida Jean always gave her the old ones from the beauty shop. Sometimes she cut out pictures for her bulletin board. She had new pictures of Betty Grable and Clark Gable cut out, ready to add to her collection.

As she walked down the hall, she paused in front of the mirror. She put down her book on the table and pulled up her hair, bringing the curls down on her forehead. There's no way I'm going to look like a movie star, she thought. She moved from one position to another and looked at herself in the mirror. There's one good thing that I have though, she thought—small ears that lie flat against my head. Her father called them elf ears when he was teasing her. Not every girl can pull back her hair because her ears are not pretty, she thought, but mine are, and maybe someday...

About four o'clock Miss Wheeler and her grandmother pulled up in front of the house. They had both been music majors at Converse College, and they had taught music for years. Several years ago, the two women had decided to live together in the Wheeler family home in Spartanburg. Claire's grandmother had made a good decision, realizing that she and Lutrell were less and less compatible.

"Only a saint could live with Lutrell," she said, "and I'm no saint. I'll be glad when Tom Ray comes back. She needs a man around the house."

Claire did not miss her grandmother when she left. She hated to hear the arguments that her mother had with her. When her grandmother visited, she was somewhat subdued, but she never forgot to remind her daughter that she had married too young and had never grown up.

Claire heard her grandmother open the door and call her mother. She heard her mother answer. She decided to give the two of them some time together before going in. She might even wait until she was called. She liked to hear her mother call her name. When she yelled out "Claire," she put extra syllables in it so that it sounded like "Clay-uh." She was named for her grandmother, and if her mother became really excited, she called her Claire Virginia. She kept on reading *Eight Cousins* until she heard her name. She went in quickly, determined to show her grandmother that she was well behaved. The book stayed on the bench in the arbor, a rose stem used as a bookmark.

She went into the living room, where they were sitting. Claire always dreaded being asked if had a piece to play. Since both women taught piano, she felt doubly threatened. She tried to avoid looking at the spinet and the picture of Jenny Lind; she didn't want to encourage an invitation. It was still summer, and she was on vacation from piano practicing.

"Claire, how nice you look," Miss Wheeler said.

"Thank you." Claire stood beside her mother. She never felt at ease with her mother, but today she felt that she had an ally against these straight-backed women with white hair and glasses.

"Come to your grandmother."

Claire walked over and let her grandmother kiss her. She stood stiffly beside her, hoping that she could escape soon.

"Aren't you feeding this child, Lutrell?" Her grandmother pinched her arm.

"I try to, Mama. She's skinny just like old Minerva Godwin. You know how the Godwins eat everything and never gain an ounce." She looked at Claire as if she were a scrub calf not fit for market. "Go get lemonade, Claire. Charlie Mae left more in the Frigidaire."

Claire was glad to leave. Coming back, she heard her grandmother say, "And that's not the worst part. She was seen at a roadhouse in Easly, and while her husband is off fighting for his country. Imagine that."

"Now, Mama, you're too hard on Cousin Emily."

"She brought the gossip on herself," Miss Wheeler said, her green eyes snapping behind her glasses.

When Claire came in, they smiled and began talking about how hot the summer had been.

"Can you stay for supper, Miss Dot?" Lutrell asked. "You know we'd be glad to have you. I enjoy so much having a visit from you and Mama."

"No, honey I have to go over to the Taylors for supper. We're all going to the wedding tomorrow at Sullivan's Island—you know that nice Murrel Hinsley is marrying that young sailor from Savannah."

When Claire left, she could hear them talking again about Cousin Emily. Her grandmother began again in a lower tone. "And anyway there's no way that baby could be Jack's. It's just a terrible thing when one of our kinspeople has just forgotten all sense of decency."

Claire sat on the stairs, where she couldn't be seen. It was like being in a movie, she thought, to hear such news. She was a little scared. Next week when her mother went to the beauty parlor, Ida Jean would be talking about Cousin Emily and her wild life.

At supper her grandmother looked up from her chicken salad and asked Claire what she'd been doing lately.

Claire looked at her mother and then back at her grandmother. "We went to a picture show in Charleston yesterday."

"All the way to Charleston? What's wrong with the picture show here?"

She looked at Lutrell. "It was a Bette Davis movie, Mama. You know how I love Bette Davis."

"Oh, so do I, Grandmother. What was really fun was walking to the picture show from the car. There were all these sailors—some even from England—on the street, and they said things to Mama."

"Is that right, Lutrell?"

"It was nothing, Mama. Claire Virginia exaggerates."

Claire looked at her mother and then at her grandmother. She did not exaggerate. She was just making conversation at the supper table.

"When Claire and I go to Charleston, and we don't go often, I take Mrs. Thomas with us. You know she always likes to get a ride to her son's house right there on Meeting Street." She looked very hard at her daughter.

Claire stopped her fork in mid-air. It was just like a movie—seeing her mother act.

She told such good lies, and her grandmother would never know the truth unless she went to the Beauty Box and talked with Ida Jean.

Going Back

This was her last day. The town was familiar to her even after a long time. A long time seemed the way to say it. She saw time as a kind of rubber band that stretches and stretches then pops back. This was a time of popping back. She needed to know what had gone before, and she needed visual messages rather than old stories. She wanted to feel what they must have felt by being where they were, little knowing who they were —pictures in albums of serious people who could not have been that serious.

The stories she knew: the piano that had been sent from Philadelphia, the tutor who taught the children French, the hunting parties with the governor, the slaves burying the silver, Sherman's men surrounding the house at twilight, and difficult times that no one wanted to remember. There were a few who still talked of the big war and what it did to the family as if there had been no other wars. Basically, they shared a feeling of loss, which increased through the years and served as an explanation for events which they could not explain. A name that went with the slaves who left, a name that mingled with other names, a name that drifted like dandelions catching to places and holding for a short while and moving on —that was the kind of name she had.

The house she remembered. One dirt road turned off another and led into pine woods. It was cool under the trees, needles bedding down the road. There was a creek which flowed through the woods, a dark, forbidding creek with lily pads year after year covering more and more of the surface until the effect was a tapestry in green, black, and white, covering untold lore. The road led into the yard, a yard without grass, a yard swept clean by brooms made from tree switches. It was hard like pavement, but a wind could toss the surface and whirl the sand about. The house was the color of rails, gray and seamed. She wondered if it had ever been painted. Often these homes in the pine woods were left to the weather as unadorned monuments. There were columns across the front, as many other houses had; a center hall led to the back of the house, where a kitchen stood apart from the house. Nothing made the house distinctive in any way except the fact that no one in her family owned it any longer. It had been valuable because it was possessed not because it was desirable.

She stopped in front of the Court House. Certainly, very few county seats could boast of such an extraordinary structure. It was settled in the center of a full block, paths crossing and intertwining. She had never

23

seen the monument at a close distance. A gardener was working on the grass, which sent runners out into the paved walks. She moved carefully on the grass, trying somehow not to disturb the grass or the gardener. The statue of the soldier had been placed there by the United Daughters of the Confederacy, and the plaque read, "In sacred memory of those who believed and died for their belief." Did they really know their belief? She needed some answers. Looking at the gardener bent over his work, she wondered what kind of beliefs he had as he pulled weeds beside the Confederate soldier. How far back did he want to go? He could be the son of a slave, perhaps even the son of one of their slaves. She turned away and walked back to the car. Her hands tight on the wheel, she looked back at the soldier and then at the gardener. Both seemed hard and impenetrable, as if made of the same substance.

The clock on the bell tower told her that it was 10:30. She needed to hurry if she was going to find the house. A few blocks led her from town, and then she was on the road—a road now paved. The road was the road she wanted, but it was not the road she knew. She didn't recognize the newly built brick houses that dotted the roadside. They signaled a kind of anonymous prosperity which had taken over the area. The cotton fields had become pastureland for cattle, and there were no people. It was a faceless countryside. She met no other cars on the road, and the only sound was that of her own car. The herds of cows were watching and grazing as she moved by them.

Where the road turned off to the plantation, there was now a sawmill. It seemed out of place there beside the road. It was a brutal force at work in a peaceful setting. When she pulled in and stopped, a worker came over to the car. Probably in his forties, he looked older. When he spoke to her, he showed a few teeth yellowed by long use of chewing tobacco. Perhaps he had some connection with them. The fact that he was there gave him some connection with them. Could they have come to this after all?

"Good morning. How do I get back to the house behind the sawmill here?"

He looked back through the woods and then pointed to a house at the crossroads. "Just go on up the road to that house up yonder on the left. Drive in the yard and follow the road around the barns.   Keep on going until you get around the head of the swamp. Then you'll be there. Nobody lives there now, you know." He looked at her and wondered why she wanted to go back.

She understood his unspoken question and answered. "Some of my people used to live there," she said, and thanked him.

She followed the road through the yard and around the barns. No one was around, and she decided not to stop to ask for further instructions. The road was just wide enough for her car, and once she passed the area of the barns and the lots the road became high with underbrush. A field of beans edged the road, and she looked out over a wide expanse of green. The noise beneath her car reminded her of a dull mower, just pressing down the weeds.

As she rounded a curve, she saw a tenant house, bigger than most of the cabins she usually associated with plantations. An empty porch across the front stood in mute testimony to an emptiness that was shut in by doors and shutters. The field had surrounded the house, as in a military maneuver, cutting off supplies from the outside. Surrender was long in coming, but it had come. She wanted to get out to walk around a little; there might be some leftovers of life there, but she would have to walk through high grass to get up to the house. She feared what might be in the grass. Her security came from being inside the car, and she wanted to maintain it. The noise of the engine gave her confidence in her mission although, as yet she didn't need it.

It was the kind of house that white farmers rented from the land-owner, probably to run on shares. When she was a child, some girls used to ride the school bus with her each morning. They were much older, but she remembered a high school girl named Ernesteen, who could draw anything. Sometimes she was late walking from the bus to her classroom because she was admiring the pictures that Ernesteen had drawn. Where had the years taken Ernesteen and her pictures? Had she made the final surrender, too?

She put the car in gear and moved on. What was it that brought her back? She wondered what kind of person would drive through this undergrowth to find a deserted house gradually giving way to the forest. Perhaps the sawmill worker had meant this house rather than the big house. Yet she hadn't thought to ask him. Sometimes she wondered why she didn't think things through more before she became involved.

The road turned somewhat to the left and she could see patches of water through the interstices between trees and bushes. Close by the car, goldenrod and chicory grew, dusty and dry in the sun, which grew hotter as she moved on, demanding more of her strength. The swamp was there just as the man had said, and she began to feel better. Perhaps coming back was not such an ill-conceived plan after all. Why shouldn't she want to see a place that they owned a hundred years ago? The house could be gone in a few years; it could be gone now.

She tried to imagine the life that they led; a life bounded by water and trees and fields. They had transplanted the accoutrements of civilization to inhospitable surroundings and maintained them with slaves. There was a cemetery for them and for their slaves, marking their interrelationship even in death, an interrelationship now elemental rather than memorial. Did they hear the silence of the land or the sound of the forest? They must have passed along this same road going to other plantations, to the county seat, to church, to the capital, and to the war. No one had been on this road for a long time, and soon there would no longer be a road. A road must take people somewhere; there is no need to go to emptiness. The road seemed to be resisting her passage more than before, and the sun, bearing down on the car, reminded her of the time that was passing. Not one of their women would be out in the middle of the day traveling; they always left while the dew was still wet in the morning and came back at twilight.

Somewhere she had read that roads in this area of the state had to have trees blazed often to keep them marked. There was always the inordinate hunger of the forest to close up its wounds and cover them over. The field stretched out, both inviting and denying her, a green lake washing against the trees.

She began to think that if something happened to her car, she would have to walk out. What kind of explanation could she give for trespassing? Did anyone see her come in? She looked closely into the woods, thinking that hostile eyes might be following her. The car no longer gave her the protection that she needed. She wanted to find the house and leave, but she was still seeking the prize but no longer confident of the terms. Today wasn't the only day she might come; perhaps someone could come with her the next time.

The road seemed to improve, leaving the field edge and turning into a grove. It was wider and hard packed, pine needles covering it. An open gate beckoned her to drive through; it was a sign, a welcome sign that she had been needing. She felt a sense of discovery as she drove slowly through the trees. This must be the road to the house; gates marked entrances.

For the first time she was able to imagine them and their connection with this gate. Little boys must have left buggies to open the gate and then close it as their fathers waited for them. Little boys probably walked from the house to this gate to sit with their legs hanging down, waiting for their fathers. Perhaps this was the gate that one little boy was swinging on as Sherman's men pulled out. A soldier had come back to him and told him where the crippled mules had been left so that he and his mother could have one for plowing. The gate marked an ending and a beginning.

The house must be there. It had to be there. The gate extended the credibility of its existence. Her eyes strained to see through the trees. There must be an opening in the trees for the house. She drove slowly, trying not to overlook anything. The trees spread over her, keeping out the sun. It was cool here although it was late morning.

She followed the road through the trees and came out abruptly into another field, where the road ended. There was no trace of a road for her to follow. She looked carefully, the car waiting for her next command. The

26

road had become a series of corn rows. The dirt was now sand, and she could feel the car sink as she tried to turn around. She had come so far to be driven back. The sand clung to the tires, and the motor raced as she tried to turn around. Looking for the road she had taken, she thought she would recognize it by the weeds she had mowed down. They should stay down for a while. She took a turn and followed the edge of the field; when she didn't come to the gate, she knew that she had made a wrong turn. She stopped, her head resting for a few minutes on her arms over the wheel.

"Oh, my God, don't leave me here. I've got to get out." She held the steering wheel tightly in her hands and began to feel somewhat stronger. She reversed slowly and started back. Another fork in the overgrown area presented itself to her, and she took it willingly. Carefully, she followed the route, and then she saw the gate. Leaving the grove, she felt she had no more choices to make, only a resolution to continue.

The fields were there, and there was the road with the weeds bowing a little toward her. The tenant house was on her left, and she could see the barns up ahead. She was coming out, and the nearer she came to the house the calmer she became. She began to feel better, trying not to think of that moment of panic when she missed the turn. She moved slowly through the yard and passed the barns and the house. No one was around in the yard, and she was too exhausted to stop and ask any questions. Perhaps she didn't really want to know the answers that might be given.

She had gone back, and there was nothing to go back for. As she drove into town, she began to think that she had gone back to herself and found something that steadied her and something that frightened her, and she was not sure that she had wanted either. The Court House clock was striking twelve as she drove past. The soldier still stood guard, and the gardener was leaning up against him eating his lunch. She knew where she was going now, and she wouldn't be going back.

Coming to Conclusions

You may wonder about my name: Marvel. Not the kind of name for a girl, I know. I've asked Mama over and over again about my name. She always says the same thing. "When I told your daddy that I was having a baby, he said, 'Marvelous, just marvelous.'" I wonder about that. I never heard a man say "Marvelous, just marvelous," but then I've never been away from Buena Vista. Certainly, I never heard it at Mrs. Cameron's boarding house, where we're living until my daddy gets back from the war.

Most of the people at the boarding house are women, but there is Mr. Folger, who is 4F, but I can't see anything wrong with him. He works at the telephone company, and I think he's sweet on Miss Lassiter, who runs McCrory's. I told Mama what I thought, and she said, "Their relationship is strictly platonic." My mother talks like that because she went to college. I used to ask her what words mean, but now I just repeat what she says whether I understand them or not.

I like to go down to McCrory's and wander through the aisles, ending up in Miss Lassiter's office in the back. She always has time for me, and we talk about life. She has encouraged me to be a reporter because I like to know all the news.

I always wonder how the girls know when to bring jacks to school, and the next day everyone is playing jacks. I'm really good at jacks. I told Mama I was planning to be a jacks champion when I grew up, but she said jacks was not a lifetime sport. It could be. I know it could be. Sometimes I play with Mrs. Cameron on the back porch when she takes a break from cooking. She'll say something like "There's nothing better than a cup of strong coffee and a game of jacks with a pretty little girl." When we take a break from jacks, we read Brenda Starr and talk about Hank and Basil. I told her I wanted to be another Brenda Starr, and she said, "We redheads have to stick together to get the news."

Mama calls Mrs. Cameron the Wife of Bath. I asked her why, and she said, "She's fat, has red cheeks, and tells stories all the time." I know other ladies like Mrs. Cameron, but Mama just calls them by their regular names. Mama told me not to puzzle over The Wife of Bath because I would meet Chaucer one day. Now I have more to puzzle over. Mama is like that, always giving me answers that are not answers at all.

Last night we had two new people, Miss Sheridan and Doris. I sat next to Miss Sheridan. She's a big, tall woman who wears glasses. Doris is

29

going to start seventh grade next week. She's not friendly at all, maybe because I'm in second grade. I can't decide if she's stuck-up or just sad.

Mama could hardly eat for asking Miss Sheridan questions. Sometimes she's embarrassing and I chew slowly and look at pictures over the buffet. I like those bird pictures. Mrs. Cameron told me that an artist named James Audubon came down south and painted those bird pictures.

Mama found out that Miss Sheridan came from North Carolina, and she works for social services. Doris is not her daughter, just a girl waiting for placement.

When we got back to our room, Mama said, "I bet that woman is lying. Doris is probably her daughter. Some man skipped out on her. It happens all the time."

I began to feel sorry for Doris. I looked over at my daddy's picture. I was glad I had a daddy, and he was fighting the Japanese. I wish he would write me though. Mama says he's too busy killing Japs to write to me. She reads little notes to me from her letters. I don't remember my daddy at all. I look at his picture and try to make up stories about him. Mama said once that he was in the navy before Pearl Harbor. That picture is all that she has, and she doesn't like for me to ask questions. She calls me "Little Miss Brenda Starr." I want to write for newspapers when I grow up. Still, I would like to have my own letters from my daddy.

People in my class get letters from their daddies, and sometimes they come home on furloughs to see them. They look so handsome in their uniforms. I have to admit I'm jealous. I want to be part of their families.

Mama will say, "Just look at those men showing off. They're not real heroes, not like your daddy." I still want to see men with their families. Sometimes my friend Eunice will invite me over when her daddy is home. She knows that I want a family. My mother always says, "We're a family, Marvel, just you and me." One time I asked, "But what about Daddy?"

She looked really serious and said, "You know, Marvel, heroes sometimes die in battle. We have to be prepared for that and be brave. That's what he would want." I know that, but I try not to think about it. I know he's coming home.

I sometimes wonder why we stay with Mrs. Cameron. Mama says it's to save money so that we can buy a house after the war, but I think it's because we have no place to go. We lived with my grandmother until a year ago, but now she's gone. She was the only grandparent I ever knew. I sometimes think of Mrs. Cameron as my grandmother. I don't tell Mama that.

Mama doesn't have a real job, just two days a week at the library. She could have a job though. She went to college. She was going to be a writer until she had me. She tells me that all the time. I talked once with Eunice about money, and she told me her mother gets allotment checks from her daddy. When I asked my mother about allotment checks, she said, "Of course, I get them. How do you think we get along?" She left me in our room before I could ask any more questions and went out to the porch.

Mr. Folger and Miss Lassiter go out walking before supper, and Mama sits on the porch and waits for them to go into the dining room. She always sits with them. I just squeeze in anywhere, and Mrs. Cameron spots me and brings in my milk. Doris and I are beginning to sit near each other now. We smile at each other.

She's not stuck-up. I found that out when Mrs. Cameron and I were playing jacks yesterday afternoon. Doris was standing in the doorway.

"Come on in, Doris. I have to leave Marvel to work in the kitchen. You take my place."

Doris smiled. "I haven't played jacks in a long time. You're probably a lot better than I am, Marvel."

"Oh, I don't know." "We played to a draw. Doris knows how to play jacks very well.

"How long will you be here, Doris?"

"Not long. I'm being placed at the end of the week with a family in Norcross."

Tonight, when I sat with Doris, my mother kept talking to Miss Lassiter and Mr. Folger, but she was staring daggers at me. Back in the room she told me that she didn't want me to associate with Doris anymore.

"Why, Mama? She's very nice to me. We played jacks this afternoon after Mrs. Cameron left for the kitchen.

"I don't want you around the likes of Miss Sheridan and her daughter."

"She's not her daughter," I said softly.

"What was that?

"Nothing."

Mama told me to get ready for bed, and she went to the porch to sit with Mr. Folger and Miss Lassiter. I wish I could sit with them, too. They both tell such interesting stories, but they're no match for Mama, who tells stories that are even better. I never know what her next story will be. Sometimes I wonder if they're true, but Mr. Folger and Miss Lassiter always enjoy them. They're both very nice to me and give me money to take to school on Mondays for my savings stamps.

On Monday nights I get ready for bed, and Mama tunes the radio to Lux Theater. Sometimes I fall asleep before it's over, but usually I listen to the end. Tonight, for some reason I began to listen to the porch conversation rather than the radio. They sat in the rockers, smoking, as they talked. I crawled over to the window to hear better.

31

Miss Lassiter said, "Oh, Cora, we're so sorry. When are you going to tell Marvel?"

"I don't know. They're so close, you know."

Mr. Folger said that he appreciated being taken into Mama's confidence. "I can see why you don't want everyone to know, especially Mrs. Cameron."

"Thank you, Jim. I know I can count on you to keep it quiet. Mrs. Cameron is such a gossipmonger."

"How long have you known that he is missing in action?" Miss Lassiter asked.

"The telegram came several days ago, and I've been preparing Marvel."

"You are so brave, Cora, so brave," Mr. Folger said.

I began to cry, and I went back to my pillow. This time I thought that I would just wait to see if Mama would tell me anything. I already knew, and I didn't need to hear more. I couldn't do anything about it.

I began to think about Doris. Now we both needed a daddy. I kept hearing Mama tell me not to associate with her. I made a plan to talk with Mrs. Cameron.

On my way to school this morning, I went through the kitchen, where Mrs. Cameron was washing up. I told her what Mama had said, and she said that she would talk to her. "It's only a few days before Doris leaves, and she needs a friend right now."

I felt better as I walked to school. I wanted to see Doris after school and play jacks again. I would be sorry to see her go. She seems real to me. My daddy is just a picture.

This afternoon I walked home, hoping that Mrs. Cameron had worked things out for me. When I opened our door, Mama pulled me in.

"That Wife of Bath thinks she can interfere in our lives. I'll show her." I looked around our room. She was packing the last bag. Daddy's picture went on top of my clothes. I held my notebook against my chest and checked my pocket for my jacks. I knew I'd never skate to school or play jacks with Doris. I would never become Brenda Starr. I would never see Mrs. Cameron again, but she was standing at the end of the hall when Mama closed our door. I turned to go to her, but Mama caught my arm and dug in her nails.

The taxi was waiting. The driver took our bags. I looked at Mama. I wanted to cry out "Where are we going and how will Daddy find us?" But I didn't.

The Waiting Game

Sarah opened the refrigerator and began taking out things, placing them on the counter and the kitchen table. She always spent a little time throwing out and rearranging after her mother left. Not once had she ever discussed the refrigerator with her mother, but they both knew that the interior of the old Frigidaire was a battlefield.

As she worked, she thought about her grandmother's funeral last week in Claxton. The family met at her Aunt Lucy's. They trailed in— her mother, her uncle Tom and her sister Marge and her brother-in-law Jim—and slowly took over the empty rooms and filled up the sink with glasses and cups. They sent out for meals and ate picnic style in front of the television. Lucy was no cook and proud of it. They wandered through the weekend, occasionally pulling away from their own disjointed lives to speak of her grandmother, who came into the world and left it without ever wondering why she had come. They envied her.

After two days, her mother, tired of the randomness of life in another house, announced, "Lucy, I don't know how you can bear to have that refrigerator in the mess it's in."

Lucy looked at her over the top of a beer glass. "If it bothers you, Sybill, clean it up."

Tom, their younger brother, suddenly awake from a doze, looked up and gave a cheer. "Get her, Lucy. Get her, Lucy, the way you used to."

Sybill turned back into the kitchen, and they could hear her working in the refrigerator.

Tom settled back in his chair and laughed. "You girls have some mama. I remember how she used to cut the rug with your grandmother. She used to slip out at night and go to dances. She was a wild one, all right." He looked at Jim. "You might have made a mistake marrying into this family, Jim. You know what they always say about girls turning out like their mothers."

Jim laughed. "There's not much chance that Marge and Sarah will ever turn out like their mother. No would could." Everyone laughed.

Lucy went into the kitchen to get more beer. Sarah followed her in, offering to help her mother with the refrigerator.

"I don't need any help from you. Go on back to the living room."

Sarah didn't wait for her to change her mind. She had offered. No one else bothered to offer. Somehow, she felt responsible for her mother and her behavior.

After the funeral she and her mother went to Sarah's apartment in Savannah. Her mother usually stayed for a week, and Sarah never encouraged her to stay longer. Arrangements were usually made with another family member or friend to come down to Savannah on some pretext in order to take her back to Waynesboro.

This last visit wasn't too bad, but the long night talks tired Sarah so much that she hated to get up for work and leave her mother to do whatever mothers left alone in daughters' apartments do. She wanted to take her mother out to dinner at least once (just to change the setting for her grievances if nothing else), but her mother, true to her nature, rejected the offer.

"Why dress up to go to a place you can't afford? I'm sure we can find something here. We'll just be two old bachelor girls spending an evening at home."

Sarah hated it when her mother used that term. When her father died five years ago, her mother became more married than ever, more involved with the intricacies of domesticity. After her grandmother died, her mother was ready to establish herself as the queen mother of the family. Even while they were gathered for the funeral, she never failed to announce to anyone who'd listen that she was seventy years old, the grand dame of the family. She couldn't understand that no one cared —not her daughters or her brother and sister. She wanted the allegiance that primitive tribes give to a ruler with life-and-death powers.

In Sarah's apartment she established herself easily and talked on and on, night after night, recounting the times she had sacrificed herself for others. Sarah knew all the stories.

"Why, the times I've bailed out that brother of mine. When he left Mildred in '49, I gave him a roof over his head and a weekly allowance until he could get himself straight." She never mentioned that six months later he was back with Mildred, cheerfully hating his sister. The price she had exacted was too high.

Sarah would sit, half-asleep, the waves of her mother's voice rolling over her and then washing out to sea. Her mother hardly needed a response from her, but sometimes she would yawn or insert a non sequitur just to see if Sybill would vary her performance. As the evening became unbearable, Sarah would get up and begin to turn out lights, finally interrupting her to say goodnight. She never kissed her mother. She had learned to withhold this token of obeisance when she was a child.

With her mother gone, she had the nights to herself. As she worked in the kitchen, she listened to the radio, tuned to a 24-hour rock station. While her mother was with her, Sarah would sometimes turn on the radio just to drown out her mother's voice.

Her mother would move to the radio. "Do you mind if I turn off this noise? It seems a shame to have on the radio when I hardly ever get to talk with you."

"Of course, Mama, whatever you say."

Then her mother would take a cup of coffee and go to the kitchen table and begin her recital of past deeds. Sarah sometimes thought of her as a wandering minstrel singing of wars and wicked events.

"You know, Sarah, I remember that cashmere sweater I bought years ago, and you wanted it so badly that I had to give it to you. Do you remember it? It was peach-colored. You wore it everywhere, remember?"

"No, Mama, I don't remember it."

Of course, she did. She was in high school then. Her mother came home with the sweater, tried it on, and offered it to her. "I don't need a sweater. You can have it. Where would I wear it? I never go anywhere to wear a cashmere sweater. This is for a young girl, Sarah. Just take it."

There was no way to refuse her. She took the sweater. A few weeks later her mother humiliated her in front of a neighbor.

"You know how it is with children. Take Sarah here —I got this peach-colored cashmere sweater the other day for myself— I hadn't bought anything for myself in so long and then Sarah just begged and begged for it. And I had to give it to her. You know how children are." She looked at Sarah and smiled.

Sarah left the room as soon as possible before she heard any more about her undeveloped sense of gratitude. The two women settled in for a long discussion of filial ingratitude. After that, the cashmere sweater lay wrinkled in the bottom of a drawer.

The kitchen set right, Sarah walked into the living room, now beginning to go back to its accustomed appearance. While her mother was in the apartment, Sarah kept things straight. If she didn't, she knew what was coming.

"You really ought to make an effort, Sarah. Our houses are expressions of our ourselves. You ought to be able to ask anyone in at any time and know the place will be neat."

Sarah thought about the years she had spent at home, where everything was neat, but no one came in. She wondered if her mother ever had a visitor except for the occasional family member. When she lived at home, Sarah never wanted anyone to come to see her, afraid that her mother would spoil any possible friendship.

She pulled a few books from the shelf and settled down to read. She read a little from each one and then decided not to read. The books stayed on the floor. She looked at the telephone. A week with her mother and then no word. Sarah knew that Sybill left unsatisfied. Sarah would not agree to leave her job and return to Waynesboro.

For several years her mother had played games with her family and friends and won time after time. If things were not going her way, she retired to her bedroom and then put out the call that she was dying. By the time everyone had assembled grudgingly around her bed, she was bright and talkative and as imperious as ever. The last time she took to her bed, Sarah was called at work. She drove to Waynesboro and stayed a week. Then she told her mother that she had to go back to Savannah. Her mother began to cry.

"It's the way of the world, Sarah. What does the world care if a mother is dying when the payroll needs to go out?"

"Mother, you're not dying. The doctor couldn't find anything wrong with you. Mrs. Barnes can look in on you. She said she would. In fact, she offered, and she's right next door."

"I don't want to rely on strangers, Sarah, when I have family."

"Mrs. Barnes has known you for years. She'll check on you. I have to get back to Savannah."

That was the same year that Marge had run off to marry Jim. The news brought on a relapse, and the family gathered at her bedside again, but they didn't have their hearts in it

In the kitchen late that night Sarah and her uncle and aunt laughed about the wedding. "You know," Lucy said, "I think the story I like best from town came from Charlene Messick, who laughed about Marge. She said that she never thought there'd be a Parsons child smart enough to outwit Sybill. She always figured that any girl who eloped would find Sybill in the trunk. She was right proud of Marge."

"I'm thinking that it's lucky that Marge could marry anybody who knew Mama. Jim is a most tolerant man, but they're going to live in Atlanta. Distance weakens Mama's power," Sarah said. She always felt closer to her aunt and uncle when they sat in the kitchen talking about her mother and wondering what she'd do next. It was like waiting for the next act of a play.

When the phone rang in Sarah's apartment, she looked at the clock. It was nine o'clock, and she was ready to watch *Masterpiece Theater*. She turned off the television.

"Sure, Aunt Lucy, I'll start out in a little while. How is she doing? What did the doctor say?" The questions were automatic, and the responses were the same. It was nothing serious now, but it could be.

Sarah put down the receiver and walked to the window. She looked down at the streetlight and thought about the warm nights she used to play hide-and-seek on her block, her father and mother talking on the front porch. She was not a survivor like her mother or her aunt or her sister. She wondered how she would end up. She didn't know if in a weak moment she would give in and go back home and live with her mother. She began to pack an overnight bag. She'd drive to Waynesboro in the morning. She called a friend at the office to tell her about the trip. There was no reason to leave tonight. She could wait. She went back to *Masterpiece*.

She packed the car at 6:00 a.m. and left for Waynesboro. When she arrived, she went up to her mother's room. Sybill was propped up with several pillows. There were some novels on the bed stand, flowers on the dresser, and a box of candy on the chest. Sarah recognized the scene.

"How are you, Mama?"

"Not so good. I had this attack yesterday just like that one back in November. You remember how that one came on. It was a Thursday, and I'd been to Augusta with Lutie Harper or was it Bessie Lambert? Well, anyway, I just got this really tight feeling in my chest and then..."

As Sybill talked, Sarah watched her mother's head grow larger and larger. She backed away from the bed and felt for the door. She had waited long enough.

Naming Names

"Your mama's got a new job, Claire, working at Walgreen's in Augusta." Her grandmother was sitting at her desk in the hall reading the letter from Lutrell when Claire walked in from school.

"What does she do, Grandmother?"

"She says she's working at the cosmetics counter. Lord knows she ought to be able to sell paints and powders. She's used enough in her lifetime." She folded the letter and put it in the letter holder and then turned to Claire. "I guess it's better than being a waitress anyway. That was real hard on her there for awhile."

"I guess so."

"Well, another Friday. How was school?"

"It was a good day. I got up front and said the *The Song of the Chattahoochee*, just the two verses we had to learn, not the whole thing. I was good, too. Mrs. Dwelle said so when I sat down." She smiled and waited for her grandmother to say something.

"Lutrell was always good with verses, too. Maybe you picked up some talent from her." She moved into the kitchen, stopping to pick up her pocketbook off the sofa. "It's getting near four already. Now go comb your hair and brush your teeth so we can go downtown. Ida Jean hates it when I'm late for my hair appointment."

Claire put her books down on the window seat and walked over to the hat rack and looked at herself in the mirror. She was wearing a long black-and-white checked skirt and a school sweater, the kind you could buy in stores and pretend you were on a team or sang in the glee club although everyone knew you were just a sixth grader. That fall the hemlines had dropped, and Claire had to have the long skirts. She was lucky to have a grandmother who believed in deep hems. For days she watched her rip out threads and throw skirts and dresses in her direction.

"If you have to be stylish, we'll try to be stylish. You're just about the most clothes-conscious girl I ever saw," she told her. "Pretty is as pretty does," she added, taking some pins out of her mouth and sticking them into the hem. She had to put facings on some of the clothes, and she told Claire not to let her hems turn over. "At least we don't have to sew on ruffles or different colored pieces like some of these dresses have."

The black-and-white skirt had been new for September, and Claire had picked out the material and watched her grandmother sew it on her treadle machine. No matter how hot it was, the girls always wore new clothes and oxfords to school. Claire hated her Girl Scout oxfords— the shoes she tried on and bought every year in Charleston. She and her grandmother and the clerk took turns peering down the machine and looking at her blue bones.

"You need string-up oxfords for your fallen feet, Claire. I never heard of anyone in our family with fallen feet. Your feet are so narrow, too. Whoever heard of a quad on a little girl?"

"Mama says narrow feet are the mark of a lady."

"Your mama has narrow feet, and she's no lady," her grandmother snapped.

Claire's faced turned red, and she felt she deserved the reproof.

From the back of the house came her grandmother's voice. "Are you ready yet?" Claire grabbed her books and ran upstairs. She always enjoyed going to the beauty shop because she liked to hear the gossip that no one thought she understood. She half-read the movie magazines and listened while Ida Jean and her grandmother exchanged morsels of news. Claire didn't want to think about her mother working in Augusta. She didn't want to ask if Johnny had left her. Maybe he had. Maybe that's why she had to get another job. Maybe he had beaten her and taken all her money. She had never seen Johnny. Her grandmother told her that he was a common sort who was 4-F during the war and nothing that Lutrell needed. But Charlie Mae said that Lutrell only needed one thing and Johnny had it. She knew that Charlie Mae shouldn't talk that way about her mother, but Charlie Mae had been with them so long that she had opinions on everybody who came into the house. She had taken care of Lutrell from the time she was born, and she didn't take much from her.

"Come on, Claire. I haven't got all day for you to while away." She ran downstairs and out onto the porch. Her grandmother closed the door and then felt down into the mailbox. She always thought she had overlooked some special letter when she picked up the mail the first time.

When they arrived at the beauty shop, Claire said that she thought she'd walk over to the McCrory's for a few minutes.

"If you see Sarah, find out if she's going to be around for the week-end. She said something about going to Charleston earlier."

Claire was glad to have an excuse to talk with Sarah, who managed the store. A dime store was one of Claire's favorite places. She liked to wander up and down the aisles looking. She had always liked picking out things and talking about her selections. "When she was no more than a baby, she was always dragging around a Sears Roebuck catalogue and talking about what she liked," her grandmother told Ida Jean one afternoon at the shop.

She saw Sarah at the cash register. "Claire, what can I sell you today?" Ever since Sarah Lambert came to town to manage the store, she had lived with Claire and her grandmother in the big house on Randolph Street. She fixed her own breakfast and then took dinner with them. Claire always admired her taste in gowns and robes. "Doesn't Sarah have the most beautiful gowns, Grandmother?" Her grandmother had sniffed and said," A lot of good they do her."

"I can't buy anything, Sarah, but I was wondering when the skates are coming in.

You promised me a pair in the very first shipment." Claire had dreamed of skating along the sidewalks for several years, but she had no chance of getting skates until after the war. Some of her friends had picked up skates form older brothers and sisters, but she had to wait. She was lucky to get a bicycle from Laura Boyer, who was away at college and didn't use hers anymore.

"You're the first on my list, honey. You have my word." Sarah was beginning to settle into that spare look that maiden ladies have when they've given up on men. Claire couldn't remember that Sarah had ever had a date, but sometimes someone invited her to dinner when she needed to make a couple with some stray male. Nothing ever came of those pairings.

"Thank you, Sarah. I can't wait to skate down Randolph and then right on down into town. I'm going to be good. I know I will. You just wait. I might even skate right down here to the store and show you."

"I'll be waiting, Claire. By the way, tell your grandmother that I'm going to Charleston after all. Hilda Driver and I are going in for a little weekend at St. John's and some Christmas shopping." Sarah smiled and gave Claire a pat on the head.

"Have a good time. I'll tell grandmother. I guess I'd better go. Grandmother will wonder where I've been so long." She started back out to the street but crossed over several aisles to the cosmetics counter and looked at the shades of Tangee. Her grandmother said that she could use the natural shade next year but there were sixth graders already using it without their mothers' permission. She left the dime store and crossed the street. Traffic was increasing now, and she wondered if there would be a crowd at the drugstore to eat.

When she walked into the beauty shop, she saw Ida Jean combing out her grandmother's hair, and she found a place to read magazines not far from the booth. She found *Photoplay* with a Van Johnson cover and looked up the feature story. There was a seventh grade boy who looked like Van Johnson, she thought, and she wanted some pictures to put on her mirror. As she read, she kept an ear out for conversations. Ida Jean never let too many minutes go by without some.

"I sure do miss having Lutrell come in, Cousin Virginia. I could always count on her to keep up with the latest styles. She never held back from trying the new things. Why, most of my ladies just go year in and year out with the same old cut and permanent, but not Lutrell. By the way, Mama said to tell you that your suit will be ready by Christmas."

When Claire and her grandmother went over to Cousin Idella's for a fitting, they had to listen to a long recital of her problems—most of them centering around her dead husband. She kept a few rooms for traveling men and did some sewing to stay afloat. "It's just enough to get by, just enough to get by. Let me tell you, being a widow is no deal. But you know that, don't you? I had to lose Claude before he could get on at the shipyard. I know he would have, too, but, no, he had to drown drunk in the river. He had to take off on weekends to drink and fish with the riff-raff he called friends. I've had to do everything for Ida Jean with little thanks from her, too. It wasn't easy sending her to cosmetology school, but I wanted her to be able to take care of herself. The good Lord knows no man will. They'll take up with her all right, but they take off after they get a little money from the beauty shop. I never seen nobody could collect strays the way she can."

There was never any need to answer Idella. She went right on pinning and basting and talking. She was the only woman Claire had ever known who could outtalk her grandmother.

When Claire looked over at the booth, her grandmother was looking at herself in the mirror.

"Now look at your grandmama, Claire. Ain't she pretty?"
Claire nodded, and she began to put away her magazine. The Friday ritual was coming to an end.

"I hear Garrett is back in town, Ida Jean." Her grandmother always heard everything in town, especially if it had to do with her relatives or near-relatives, and she liked to check out the facts.

"Everybody's seen him but me. I guess he knows I don't want to see him without some money. When everybody closes the door to him, he'll come down the street and come in my back door."

"Garrett had a hard time in the navy. A lot of men are having a hard time making it now. Why, Faulkner called last night. He's at loose ends." Claire went back to Van Johnson, who was a lot more interesting than her Uncle Faulkner, who never seemed to be all right. His life flickered like a match in a breeze; money problems, wife problems, drinking problems.

When her grandmother paid, Ida Jean came over to Claire and told her to take some magazines. "I know how you enjoy them, honey. I got plenty here. Take a few."

Claire looked at her grandmother for permission.

"God only knows what you want with any more than you've got up there in that attic room, but take them if you want." Her grandmother called her room the movie lobby, and Claire hated to give her any fuel for her arguments. She reluctantly put the magazines back, and they started home.

On Fridays they didn't cook for the boarders, and they had decisions to make about eating. They stopped off and looked in the windows of the Band Box.

"Don't you just love the two-piece suit with the little waist and the long skirt, Grandmother?"

"It's right pretty for a thin person, Claire. You'll look good in a suit like that when you're older. You'll have the figure for it."

"I guess so," Claire answered, not knowing whether to take her words as a compliment or not. Perhaps there would be a time when a tall, thin figure would be right. It would be her luck to have the styles change before she was old enough to wear grown-up clothes.

"You ought to have one of those pillbox hats with a veil, Grandmother."

"They look nice, but I spend my Sundays at church at the organ and my weekdays in the kitchen, so I don't need fancy hats."

"I wonder how you eat with a tight veil around your mouth."

"Goodness me, Claire, don't you know that mannequins and models don't eat at all? We mortals have to eat though. Are you hungry?" They were on the same side street as the People's Pharmacy.

"Could we eat at the drugstore?"

They both laughed. They played this little game every Friday night. They walked from the beauty shop in the direction of the drugstore and then asked if they were going there to eat. They were regulars who knew everyone there.

"You know most everybody, Grandmother," Claire would say after she had been introduced to someone on the street or in a store.

"Well, I ought to. My parents and my grandparents lived right here all their lives, and I have, too, except for the time I stayed with Miss Dorothy in Spartanburg."

They went in and spoke to everyone, and moved to the last booth. Tonight it was empty and waiting.

"Do you want a grilled cheese and a coke, Claire? I believe you could live on a steady diet of sandwiches and soft drinks." Her grandmother settled into the booth, ordered a cup of coffee, and looked over the menu.

"Who is our waitress tonight?" Claire asked, looking over at the soda fountain at the young girl heading back with a cup of coffee.

"I believe that's Chancey Sparks' girl. They live out on Graybar Road."

When the waitress came over, her grandmother went directly to the problem.

"You look like one of the Sparkses."

"Yes ma'am, I am. I'm the last one, Miss Virginia. You had me in Sunday school a few years ago."

"Why, sure, I remember you now, Mary. This is my grandbaby, Claire. She's in the sixth grade and wants some skates for Christmas this year."

"Oh, Grandmother, don't tell everybody." Claire knew she was blushing. Her grandmother would take up with the devil if he had time for a little conversation. At least that's what Lutrell said about her once. Sometimes Claire agreed.

She ordered her usual, and her grandmother ordered a BLT and a scoop of strawberry ice cream for dessert with another cup of coffee.

While they waited for their meal, Claire's eyes ran over the aisles near them. She looked at the shampoo: Breck, Halo, Drene. She knew them all. She always read the shampoo ads in the magazines. She would have given anything to have long, thick, shiny hair. When she was younger, she wanted pigtails, but her hair was too thin. Once Lutrell plaited her hair and then gave her a mirror. "There, Miss Heidi, don't you look ready for the photographer?" Lutrell squealed with laughter and fell over on the bed. Claire pulled off the rubber bands and ran upstairs to her room and cried. From the shampoos she looked over at the toothpastes: Ipana, Colgate, Pepsodent, and little bottles of Teal, a red liquid for cleaning teeth. Claire had never known anyone who used Teal. At home they used Dr. Lyons powder.

"Do we need anything, Claire?"

"I don't think so." She wished she could go through the perfume section and choose some cologne, but she knew better than to ask. At Christmas she always bought some Evening in Paris for her grandmother. This year she might buy some powder, too.

She could imagine her mother standing behind the cosmetics counter, smiling at customers and giving them advice about various jars, boxes, and tubes around her. She could hear her talking about the brands she used. Everyone would take her advice very seriously because she always looked so glamorous, her blond hair waved around her face, her eyebrows plucked, her long dark lashes over wide blue eyes. Odalisque, Lutrell called them. Claire had looked up the word, and she sometimes said it slowly while she was brushing her hair at night. "Odalisque. Odalisque. My mother has odalisque eyes."

They ate their sandwiches, each concentrating on Lutrell. They began at the same time, "Do you think she's..."

"Go on, Claire."

"No, ma'am, you go ahead."

"Well, I was just wondering if your mama can come for Christmas this year. She couldn't make it last year after saying she could." She drank some coffee and looked carefully at Claire.

"Don't worry, Grandmother. It's all right if she doesn't come. She may have to work anyway." What she couldn't say was that Johnny might not let her come. Maybe that's why she didn't come last year. He knew that he would never be welcome, and he knew why. He had been living with Lutrell now for over a year with no plans to marry.

"Still and again I worry about her. You know I do." They finished their food and paid and began to walk home. Her grandmother had never learned to drive, and they walked everywhere. They walked along Eighth and then turned at the hotel and started down Randolph. The houses along this part of the street looked alike -- two stories, white, Victorian. Most of them had old people living in them. Claire was the only child in the neighborhood.

It had been three years now since Lutrell left them. Sometimes Claire relived that summer when she was eight, when she and her mother went to movies in Charleston every week, when her grandmother lived in Spartanburg with Miss Dorothy, when her father was fighting in the Pacific. By Thanksgiving her grandmother was back with them because Miss Dorothy had died; by Christmas her mother had run off with a sailor she had met in Charleston. In April when the telegram came to tell them of her father's death at Corregidor, she was unable to cry. When she listened to the radio and heard "I'll Be Seeing You" or "Together," she sometimes cried and thought of her mother and father and herself when they were living together in her grandmother's house. She remembered playing under the streetlight with her friends while her parents sat in rocking chairs on the darkened front porch. She never thought that the front porch would be empty when she looked down the street from the light.

"We forgot to turn on the porch light, Claire. Will you run up and put it on? I'm getting so old I might stumble and fall."

"Sure, Grandmother." Claire ran up the steps and opened the door. They never locked their doors. In fact, they couldn't find a key for either one of the outside doors. She stuck her hand in fast for the light, always thinking that someone was waiting to grab it before she could turn the switch. The light flooded the porch, and she held the door open. Her grandmother went in, dropped her pocketbook on the sofa, and headed for the kitchen.

"Tomorrow's going to be busy, Claire. There's the Christmas baking and then our piano lesson and then supper and then a little time to study the Bible lesson."

Claire followed her into the kitchen. "Oh, Grandmother, I forgot to tell you. Sarah won't be here for the weekend. She's going to Charleston with Hilda."

"One less to worry about, I guess."

They sat down at the table as if they expected another waitress to come out of the shadows. Claire looked around, thinking that she had spent so much time in this one room with her mother, with Charlie Mae, and with her grandmother. She liked the kitchen even though it looked old-fashioned and dingy. She looked over at the gas stove up on legs. It was green and beige. There was oilcloth on the table—a Mexican print that was beginning to wear through. Claire tried to cover the spots with dishes when she set the table. She looked at the sink by the window and thought of all the dishes she had washed and dried. Even though Charlie Mae wasn't there, it was still her kitchen. Claire and her grandmother just used it.

"Penny for your thoughts. Still thinking about your skates?"

"Oh, no, but I could with a little prompting." She smiled at her grandmother, who had the cups now for coffee. She poured a half cup of milk into Claire's cup and then filled it with coffee. There was always coffee waiting to be heated up, and her grandmother usually had a cup near her somewhere. One of Claire's jobs was to hunt up all the cups in the morning. She might find then anywhere in the house, wherever her grandmother stopped for a few minutes.

"There's nothing like a cup of hot coffee on a cool night." She sat down and fixed her coffee with two spoons of sugar. "Somewhere I heard that a true Southerner uses milk or sugar but not both, so I guess we're true Southerners." They laughed and stirred their coffee. "What kind of fruitcake do you want to make tomorrow? Light or dark? Charlie Mae is getting the scuppernong wine to pour over it."

"I like the dark best, I think. Remember last Christmas when we had ambrosia and fruitcake and eggnog?"

"It was a good Christmas, wasn't it?"

When Claire thought back, she could see her grandmother sitting at the dining room table pouring tea and coffee for her friends from church and her bridge friends. Faulkner went to his in-laws in Soperton, and there were just the two of them. Claire thought that her grandmother had planned the Christmas get-together for her because they would be less alone on Christmas Day. Her grandmother was like that. She could push herself to do really good things for people. Claire and Charlie Mae had worked for days in the kitchen to have everything just right. Her grandmother had been playing for the Christmas pageant and had enough to do with those practices and the choir practices for the midnight service.

"It was nice, Grandmother, real nice." The telephone rang, and her grandmother went into the hall to answer it.

"Not much, just having a cup of coffee." There was a long pause.

"Getting a little lonely then without him, are you?"

Claire knew that it was Lutrell. She had to be really depressed to call. As long as things were going well, she never called. Probably drinking, she thought. She had never seen her mother drink except at Christmas, but Charlie Mae said she did. Claire never questioned her because she wasn't sure she wanted Charlie Mae to tell her any more.

"No, Faulkner isn't coming, but I didn't think he would. He's not doing well either. Life's just too hard for him. What about you? Do you have any money? Can you keep the place?"

Claire knew that her grandmother would send money. She always did for Faulkner or Lutrell when they got into scrapes.

"Well, you see how it goes. If you need some, let me know. We won't count on you for Christmas. I don't want Claire to be disappointed. Don't do that to her again."

Claire felt like an object in the store window when they talked about her like that. How did her grandmother know that she would be disappointed? The more she thought about seeing her mother the more nervous she became. I won't look good enough, she thought. Sometimes when she looked into the mirror, she knew that her mother was right: she looked more and more like her father's people. Her hair had turned darker, but it was thin and wispy -- not possible for pageboys. It was cut short now, and she looked younger than her age. She was growing tall just like her father. "Straight as a pine," Charlie Mae said. She was hoping that her mother was too upset to speak with her. She never knew how to talk to her mother.

When her grandmother came back, she went to the stove, turned up the burner, and then poured more coffee. "I hate cold coffee."

"What did she say?"

"Oh, Claire, I don't know what will become of her. She talks big one minute, telling me how you should be with her in her time of need, and then again, she's crying and hoping Johnny will come back."

"Maybe he will," Claire ventured. She found it hard to visualize him. She somehow thought of him as a blond like her mother. He probably smoked camels and drank Heaven Hill. Maybe he rolled his cigarettes instead of buying packs—maybe Bull Durham in little sheets. Claire knew that he must be a tough-talking character who probably said "I taken" or I seen" or "between you and I." For all Lutrell's talk about nice people, Claire knew that she was happiest with the roadhouse crowd, else why would she have left her to go to Cousin Emily's in Easley and take up with sailors. That's what her grandmother had said about Cousin Emily. "She likes her men tough and leaning on pinball machines." Lutrell left the sailor and took up with Johnny. When Claire thought about sailors and men like Johnny, she thought about all the people in the world she didn't know and didn't trust and she was afraid that sometime she might be like her mother and go out and look for them.

"The good Lord knows, Claire. I just don't want you to be mixed up with that kind of life. I thought I'd raised Lutrell better than that, but you never know. You never know." She drank her coffee. "Did you get your skates set up with Sarah?"

"Everything is set. Can't you just see me skating up and down sidewalks and around and around the church? I think I have some talent, Grandmother. Why, if I lived up North, I would take up ice skating. I could be another Sonja Heine. I know I could."

"You probably could, child. Something for you to dream about tonight. Let's clean up this little repast as Martha said after the Last Supper."

Claire laughed. Her grandmother liked to make little jokes about Biblical characters. When she went to bed that night she saw snow and ice and a frozen lake and skaters coming out in different colors, their skates flashing in the afternoon sun. The last couple glided by her, and she recognized her mother with Van Johnson.

"Come on, Claire, hurry up," Lutrell called to her.

"I'm coming, Mama. Wait."

Family Receipts

As she rounded the curve, she saw the ocean and knew that coming to the island was a good idea. Her sister Margo was waiting for her, and Bitsy almost expected Aunt Billie to be waving a handkerchief over the porch railing. Before her death, Aunt Billie always rented this particular cottage. Bitsie pulled in beside the Toyota and rested for a minute. By the time she was out of her car, Margo was beside her.

"Oh, Bitsy, I'm so glad you're here." They kissed and held each other. "It's been too long, too long."
Bitsy unlocked the trunk, and Margo began laughing. Bitsy spread her arms. "I tried to bring everything. I even stopped at Piggly Wiggly on the way in."

"You old silly. Remember what Aunt Billie used to say? 'I couldn't decide what to bring, so I brought it all?' You must be exhausted. All the way from Syracuse in one day."

"There are airplanes and rental cars, Margo. I use them. Not like years ago when I'd drive straight through."

"We're getting old, honey."

Bitsy stopped at Margo's car. "When did you get this Toyota?"

"A few weeks ago. I totaled my old one. It was all my fault though. I was looking at some Christmas decorations and didn't notice the car in front of me."

Bitsy laughed and shook her head. They gathered up all they could hold and went up the stairs. They left boxes in the kitchen and took bags to the first bedroom.

"You left Aunt Billie's room for me?"

"Of course, I did. You always wanted it, didn't you?"

"Sure. Aunt Billie used to tell me, 'You have to earn this big room and this big bed.'" Bitsy walked to the window overlooking the ocean and then turned around.

Margo joined her and stuck a lit cigarette in Bitsy's mouth. "Okay, just keep on talking and walking, and you'll be just like her."

Bitsy struck a pose and waved the cigarette. "Just a fool for a cigarette."

They laughed and then they were quiet. Bitsy rubbed out the cigarette in an ashtray, and they went into the kitchen.

The counters were soon full of food and kitchen essentials. Margo began to put things in the cupboards, but Bitsy stopped her.

"Just leave these things out,' Aunt Billie used to say. 'We'll need

49

them sometime.' "

"You even sound like her, Bitsy. Remember that time you asked her why she never put things away?"

"Oh, yes. She said, 'I get paid to be organized at the post office. At home I'm on my own.'"

"I think we can dispense with that philosophy. I can't stand having all that stuff out." Margo began to sort things a little too fast. Bitsy took her hand.

"It's all right, Margo. I know it's hard for you. First Walker and then Aunt Billie. You've had a bad year."

Margo turned to her. "I'm going to be all right. I know it." Bitsy led her over to the couch. They sat side by side, sharing a cigarette, their feet on the coffee table. Bitsy took her hand. "Listen, sunshine girl, life goes on as the soap operas say."

"I thought I was prepared to lose Walker. I kept saying that I'd had a good man and a good marriage. But it wasn't enough."

"Death is not easy even if it is expected, Margo. I know. We were never ready to let Aunt Billie go." Bitsy felt the tears coming. She looked away from Margo. "Did you give Mary Lee our number?"

"I think so. Do you think she'll come tonight? She always came with Aunt Billie."

"I hope so. I think we need each other." Bitsy looked toward the kitchen. "Did you bring something to eat tonight or should we go out?"

"Whatever you think. We could always have breakfast. I brought sausage and eggs and grits. I brought flour, too. We could have biscuits and jelly. I made some quince for you."

"Why not? Sounds good to me. I don't get grits or quince jelly in Syracuse."

"I'll make the biscuits," Margo said. "I read somewhere that it's all in the flour. I've got White Lily."

"You know, I saw White Lily in a Williams-Sonoma catalogue."

"Imagine."

Margo measured out the dry ingredients and began mixing the dough. As they cooked, they began to talk about Mary Lee and the other folks, the term they used for Uncle Win's family. The two of them and their cousin Mary Lee had grown up together: the sisters with Aunt Billie and their cousin with her mother Mary Lou, who lived a few blocks from them. Uncle Win and his family still lived out on the old home place — an unpainted two-story with various trailers parked on the property.

"Children of the war. That's what Aunt Billie used to call us," Bitsy said. "When I look back, we were so lucky to have Aunt Billie."

"Oh, I know. Our daddy dead and our mother in Milledgeville. Do you remember how the school children used to rag us? 'Are you going to the asylum to see your mother?'"

"That was hard." Bitsy measured out the water for the grits. The coffee was making.

"You know what's harder is to hear about Uncle Win's family. You must hear more than I do. You're not that far from Mary Lee. She's the one to take the hit. She has to hear about them and see them."

Margo poured coffee for them. "Their lives keep the gossip mills turning. Drugs, divorces, crime, adultery, DWI's, hair-brain schemes. You name it. They do it."

Bitsy looked up. "I sometimes think about Uncle Win in uniform."

"Oh, yes. He used to write to us, remember? We thought he had won the war all by himself."

"I can see him now coming home, with Carmellia. She was so pretty, so different from us. Downright exotic."

"It was all so romantic." Margo sighed. "We had never known anyone from Texas before."

Bitsy laughed. "She's the only person I've ever known from Texas." Bitsy looked serious. She lit a cigarette. "He should have stayed in the army. He never wanted to farm, and he didn't know how to do anything else."

"I think he just wanted to please his parents. You know how Papa Hamp and Mama Julia felt about their land. He was their only son. The family name would go on."

"I sometimes think I'm too hard on Uncle Win's family. They're pitiful the way they try to live 'all whichaway' as Aunt Billie used to say. You have to admit though we never had armed robbery in our family before."

"Well, Little Win's doing his time in Pikeville. What a blessing his parents did not lived to see that."

"What about Maria? She's the cousin Mary Lee had hopes for. I know she used to give her money."

"Mary Lee thought she was helping her to learn computers, but she found out the money was going for drugs. Mary Lee's a push-over just like Aunt Billie."

"What about Aunt Carmellia?"

"She consoles herself that everything is God's will. She only goes out to church now."

They filled their plates in the kitchen and took them to the dining room. Bitsy went back for coffee. They sat down.

"Now look around, Bitsy. If you don't see something, don't ask for it. It's all out."

"Now you sound like Aunt Billie."

Margo sampled a biscuit. "It's good but not as light as Aunt

51

Billie's."

"They're really good, but I'll eat any biscuits you make. Keep trying recipes."

As they ate, the rain began. Margo looked out. "I didn't know rain was predicted."

"Flip on the Weather Channel."

Margo waited by the screen, looking out toward the ocean, and then back to the TV. "Look, Bitsy, there's a tornado warning all the way to Charleston. My God!" She went into the kitchen for more coffee. The rain pelted down. The waves hit the foundation, and the house shivered.

Bitsy smiled. "I'd forgotten how it feels in these houses on stilts."
They took their dishes back to the sink. "Let's leave these until tomorrow, Bitsy. I know you're tired." They went to their rooms and quickly returned to the hallway.

In one voice they yelled, "I didn't bring any sheets."
Bitsy went to the linen closet. "Oh, good, the owners left some really big sheets for my bed." She took the linens to her room. Margo followed and helped her make the bed.

"I didn't see any others, Margo. We'll have to share — just like we used to with Aunt Billie sometimes. There are some blankets though. I'll get them later."

They looked outside, hoping that Mary Lee was having no trouble on the road. "Maybe she's still at home, Bitsy. Why don't we call?" Margo poured more coffee, and Bitsy went to the telephone.

"Well, either she's on the road or buying us some food at the Pig. She's usually so organized, I'm surprised she hasn't called." They went to their rooms and changed. When they met in the bedroom, each holding a book, they began laughing.

"Where is our Kathleen Norris novel?" Margo asked. Aunt Billie used to tell us plots as if they were children's stories."

"When I go on vacation or go into the hospital, I have to have a stack of my happy books,' Aunt Billie used to say. Did you ever read any?"

"No, I didn't have to. I knew all the plots by heart. What are you reading?"

"I'm preparing a paper on Charlotte Yonge. Her books are long nineteenth-century Kathleen Norris novels. I can count on her."

Margo held up Mrs. Dull's cookbook. "Remember this? Aunt Billie used to swear by it."

They settled in, Margo in her well-worn red chenille bathrobe and Bitsy in men's flannel pajamas. Margo flipped through recipes, stopping here and there.

"Anything special you're looking for?"

"The perfect biscuit! I saw a recipe in the paper for Touch of Grace Biscuits, but I forgot to cut it out."

"If you're like me, you would have forgotten to bring it even if you remembered to cut it out."

Finally, Margo laid down her book. "I can't concentrate. It must be this storm. I'll try tomorrow."

Bitsy looked up over her glasses. "There's always tomorrow as they say." She placed a bookmark in *The Daisy Chain* and turned off the light. "How's Mary Lee taking Richard's marriage?"

Margo doubled up her pillow and sat up. "I guess she was all right until he and Wanda bought that big Italianate just down from the library. Now she sees them all the time."

"Just imagine. Your husband leaves you for his receptionist and then moves practically next door to the place you work. How sensitive can men be?"

"Not very. Mary Lee just keeps on stamping books and smiling. Who knows what's behind all those smiles?"

"Well, the work keeps her somewhat sane, I guess." The storm continued. Lightning played around the room. Bitsy sensed Margo's fear.

"You still hate storms, don't you?"

"Does it show that much?"

"Aunt Billie used to talk about other things with you, remember?"

"I remember but I still cried."

Bitsy wanted to distract Margo from the storm. "I saw something in the paper that Aunt Billie would have loved. The governor of Tennessee said that what corrupted people was too much money and beach houses."

Margo giggled. "Aunt Billie would say we're only semi-corrupted."

They closed their eyes and thought of their childhood visits to the island. Billie used to take them the week after Christmas every year. She said she needed a rest after the Christmas rush at the post office. Their friends thought it was odd, but the girls loved being away with her.

"You're thinking of Aunt Billie, aren't you?" Bitsy squeezed Margo's hand.

"Of course, I am. She kept us going, didn't she? She always had a new story or a crazy saying. You remember how excited she'd get talking about Uncle Win's family? She'd tick off their children and husbands and wives and lovers with the accuracy of a sportscaster. I can hear her now: Winston and Carmellia, then Little Win, Linda, and Baby Marie. She remembered Linda's three husbands and most of her boyfriends and her children Luann and Rush and Marilyn and Lyle."

"Oh, stop it, Margo."

"I can't remember as many as Aunt Billie could. You get the

picture anyway,"

"She once told me, 'They just keep coming on like fire ants, honey.'"

"Fire ants, that's good," Bitsy laughed.

There were more pauses now between their words. The rain continued. The waves were higher, and the house shook now and then.

"Bitsy?"

"What?"

"I forgot to bring you something."

"What?"

"Pecans. I picked them up myself and took them down to get them cracked. I thought we could work on them here so that you could take them back."

"It's all right, Margo.."

"Bitsy?"

"Go to sleep, Margo."

Margo listened to Bitsy's light snoring. She was used to Walker's snoring. She drifted off, comfortable with her old routines.

In the morning, the telephone ringing woke them at the same time. Bitsy looked at her watch, still thinking she had a class to teach. It was 9 o'clock.

"Who has this number, Bitsy?"

"My house sitter, Lois and Mary Lee, I guess. It better be Mary Lee. I'll get it." Bitsy ran barefoot into the living room. "Oh, Mary Lee, it's you. Are you coming?" Margo was standing next to her now.

"Let me talk to her. You what? Oh, Mary Lee, don't you ever learn? I know. I know. It's okay. Just get down here as soon as you can and bring two sets of double sheets. I forgot mine. Bitsy found some kings in the closet, and we both slept in the big bed. Drive safely now, you hear. We're wild to see you. Bye now." Hanging up, she looked at Bitsy. "I almost said, 'Give our love to Aunt Billie.'"

"What did she tell you?"

Margo began the coffee. "At the last minute she had to put Earle on a plane in Savannah."

"Who is Earle?"

"He's Little Win's boy. He's going to live with his grandparents in Alabama now that his parents are gone. I forgot to tell you that Charmaine was with Little Win on that robbery. She's in jail, too."

"What a crowd. Why Mary Lee?"

"She's probably got the only car they know that's running."

"You know, Margo, when we were children, we didn't know people like this, and now we're related to them."

"And the thing is they're tough as pine knots for all their troubles."

Bitsy shook her head. "Let's change our clothes and walk along the ocean. There's no rain now. We can check out the beach damage.

Let's take a thermos of coffee, too." She patted her stomach. "I need to take some off."

"Oh, Bitsy, we don't want to lose weight. We'd lose our pretty faces. That's what Aunt Billie used to say."

They walked toward the state park, Bitsy leading the way. She worked out a few shells with her foot and waited for Margo to catch up.

"You know, Margo, you could go back with me for a visit. I have some more time off before the semester starts."

Margo took her hand. "I'll think about it. I really will. You're sweet, Bitsy, you really are."

As they walked, they stopped and examined shells, selecting, improving, and discarding old ones. At home they already had shell collections, but there was always the hope of getting just the right ones.

Hearing the Lost Voices

"Are you sure she expects us?"

"Oh, yeah. I talked with her before I picked you up at school."

Standing on the latticed porch, the two women peer into the parlor windows and then turn back to the empty street.

"Aunt Lotte probably just stepped out for a minute. I could just walk in. I know the door is unlocked, but I don't know about the dogs Grandmother used to have.

"What kind?"

"Dobermans. Friendly but a bit demanding."

"I hate Dobermans." Ward walks over to a beefsteak begonia spilling over a woven stick basket. "Just look at this. It's huge."

"It's several generations old. My mother used to talk about watering it when she was a child."

They settle into a swing, their figures casting afternoon shadows across the unpainted floor. A few cars pass. A train rumbles by somewhere out of their view. A black cat wanders up the steps, looks at them briefly, and disappears along the side porch. They hear a car stop and then footsteps. Paige gets up. "She could be here."

A tall woman with gray hair and loose glasses, holding a heavy bag, appears, out of breath and smiling. "Why, my goodness, girls, you beat me here. I said to myself, 'if I go to the liquor store, I bet they'll show up.' I did and you did." She puts down the bag and reaches for Paige.

Ward waits to be introduced. "This must be Ward. I've heard so much about you." She enfolds Ward and motions to Paige to pick up her bag, "We'll set up the bar and get out some munchies."
She leads the procession down the hall. "Bless your hearts. All the way from New York for a conference on southern women writers. We must be doing something right." She looks back at Paige. "You could have just walked in. I never lock up."

"I didn't know about the dogs, Aunt Lotte."

"Oh, Lord. When the lawyers finally found me, I told them to get rid of those dogs before I'd come back."

"I really wish you could have made the funeral. I needed some moral support. Even if I'd known in time I wouldn't have come to meet all those harpies who would have been there to see the prodigal daughter. Well, enough of all that. You probably need to freshen up. Take Ward upstairs, Paige. Your bedroom is the blue one opening onto the sleeping porch. You may get too hot to sleep in the bedroom."

"Ward and I'll get our stuff from the car." They leave Lotte humming and setting out glasses and coasters. When they start upstairs, she calls out to Paige, "Did you see anyone you knew on the way in?"

Paige stops on the landing. "You won't believe this, Well, maybe you will. I stopped for a toothbrush at the Rite-Aid. I was standing in the line to pay, and someone came up behind me and goosed me. Then he yelled out, 'What do you say, Book?' I almost dropped my money. It was Harley Odom. He always called me book in grammar school.

"He's a sight, isn't he? He sees me sometimes and asks about you. Ward deposits her bags and wanders out to the sleeping porch. So this is a sleeping porch, she thinks. Another piece of southern exotica. All her life she has lived in upstate New York, and the South seems like a foreign country. Her first trip to Georgia seems to confirm her expectations. She marvels at Paige's ability to slip into this slow-motion world. She even begins to sound like a Southerner. Soon she'll be saying Ward with six syllables. That's how Paige characterizes an old college friend:

"Paige has four syllables when Mary Ellen calls me."

Ward stands at the rail and hears Lotte and Paige giggling like seventh graders. She goes down. "Am I missing a good story?"

"Oh, Ward, Aunt Lotte was just telling me how Mrs. Jenkins spies on her. We were standing at the window so that she could see us clearly from her bathroom."

"She is always at the ready with a window on this house." Lotte gets out the scotch. "Paige says you'll want scotch. Water or soda? Maybe you'll want to make it."

Ward makes hers and Paige's while Lotte arranges cheese and crackers. They take their drinks out to the back porch as Lotte has directed them. She brings out a table for them.

"The front porch is more comfortable, but I have to hunker down back here or the churches will be praying for me."

"Is it still that bad, Aunt Lotte?"

"For the Jezebel times never change."

Paige giggles, and Ward looks blank. Maybe Paige should have been more forthcoming, she thinks.

"What did Paige tell you?"

"Nothing much. Just that you were her favorite aunt and that you had inherited the house."

"Paige, you are a saint. As I get to know you better, Ward, I'll let out my life story in little spurts." She smiles and finishes her drink, rattling the ice and then smoothing down her skirts. "Oh, what the hell? I was married four times—what I call the unholy alliances. What's that Mae West said? 'I was snow white, but I drifted?' "

They laugh and watch Lotte mix another scotch. "These glasses are so short that I'm always having to refill them. Here, have some cheese and crackers. This is a little skimpy tonight, but tomorrow while you're at the conference I'll be more creative."

Ward and Paige smile at each other, drinking slowly and watching Lotte. She's just beginning the evening, they think.

"Paige, why don't you take Ward out to the river for dinner? On me, of course. I had a big lunch and I'm going to peel a few grapes and go to bed."

"Oh, sure. That would be fun. We were hoping to have some fish on this trip. You sure you won't go with us?"

"No, no. You remember how to get there?"

"I think so. Out 33 and hook a left at the Ebenezer Baptist?"

"That's right. You can't miss it. Here's my Visa."

"Oh, no. Keep your money, and we'll take you out before we leave."

"That would be nice..." Ward hesitates. She can't think of a last name.

"Just call me Lotte. That's what I tell Paige, but she will call me Aunt."

Paige smiles. "What name are you using now?"

"Oh, I just went back to Curtis. The old name still means something around here. I'm sixty years old, and I'm still the Curtis girl."

Lotte walks with them to the front porch, says goodbye, and empties her ice into the begonia. She waves to the possibility of Mrs. Jenkins, and then she opens the screen and goes into the dark hall.

As Paige opens the car door, Ward covers her hand and whispers, "It's going to be all right, Paige."

"I know. I know. I'll just have to get her at the right time."

Paige drives into down. "Here's the main street — Cotton Avenue. When I was a child, these stores were thriving and Saturday was like a big market day. Now, just look at all the empty buildings and the amateurish signs. See the building by the bank — my great-uncle built it. See Curtis on the stone at the top?"

Ward looks at Paige and nods. What can she say? This place looks dead and dying. She can see it without the sentimentality. Better it die and people move away. There's nothing to hold them here.

"Of course, you weren't born here. I could show you the hospital where I was born. Now it's a senior citizens' home. My school is a couple of blocks away and across the street is First Baptist, where all my family went."

She turns onto 33 at the light, and they are in the country with a few unpainted houses on each side of the road and then a cotton gin. As they meet cars, the drivers wave.

"You certainly do know a lot of people, Paige."

"Oh, I don't know any of them. They're just friendly."

The hostess at the restaurant does know Paige. "You're Miss Centy's granddaughter, aren't you?"

Paige acknowledges the connection, and the hostess takes them out to the screened porch. "It's been so hot everybody wants to sit outside. I guess we'll have to go for air conditioning next year."

Over tall tea glasses, they look at each other. Ward tells Paige they are both tired. Paige shakes her head. "Not me."

Well, we are, Ward thinks. Another semester yet to finish. Papers and more papers to grade. This April conference seemed like a great idea — southern women writers and a chance to stay in an old southern home. "The ambiance will be perfect," she remembered Paige saying.

"What did the hostess call your grandmother?"

"Oh, it's a southern nickname for Recentia — Centy. I used to think she was named for a coin."

"I never heard that name."

"I don't think anyone has. She always said that her mother used to get names out of novels.

When the meal comes, they pay attention to eating. Hush puppies, coleslaw, and catfish. Paige eats greedily as if she's been deprived too long. Ward eats carefully, not sure of the flavors. Her iced tea is hardly touched when Paige orders more.

"You're not used to sweet tea, Ward. Would you like some unsweetened?"

"No, this is all right," She looks at the river. She used to feel as if she were floating on a river, always moving, never thinking about the future. This time she has planned right. In fact, she thinks that they have planned right. She's over Tammy now, and Paige has become everything to her. This time will be right.

"A penny for your thoughts," Paige smiles.

"You, of course."

"Thank you, ma'am. Let's look at the dessert list. I have to warn you. The pies are sensational — chess, pecan, and coconut meringue. Always the same and always delicious"

"I don't think I'll indulge, and you shouldn't either. You know that we promised each other we'd lose weight this spring."

Paige looks down. "You're right." When the waitress comes, Paige orders two coffees. "I hate to give up that pie, but I have to be strong."

"Well, ma'am, that is a show of strength in the face of those pies. I applaud you," the waitress tells her.

Ward watches her until she pushes the swinging door to the kitchen. "Well, you're right about one thing — there are pretty girls in the South."

"You probably never heard the old saying – 'Southern cooking makes you good looking, have you?'"

"I can't say that I have."

"Oh, come on. You're just a push-over for a blonde. I don't know how I ever attracted your attention with my mouse-brown hair."

"It was your mind, Paige, your mind. I recognized that the first day of class when we ate together in the faculty dining room."

"I thought you were just being helpful to 'a pore girl a fur piece from home' as they say in the mountains."

"I was. I was." She pats Paige's hand. "Let's blow this joint."

On the way back, they drive by the school. "Look at that last window on the left. That was my third-grade class with Miss Burdell Morrison. I loved her. I used to walk home for lunch, and there was this country girl named Faustine, who used to save a swing for me."

"I can just see you coming on the playground demanding your swing."

"I wasn't like that. She never said a word, just slowed down, and handed me the chain."

There is a dim light in the front hall, but, otherwise, the house is dark. Next door the porch light is on, and the house is full of light. A figure moves around in the livingroom.

"Is that Mrs. Jenkins?"

"Sure. She's a nice lady. She was awfully good to me after Mama's accident. I was in college when she died. I was just lost. I didn't even know if I'd go back or not. She told me that Mama would have wanted me to."

"Are you going to visit her?"

"Oh, sure. Tomorrow afternoon when we get back, we'll go over. I know she's expecting us."

They feel their way down the hall to the kitchen light. They put ice into a bucket, pick up some glasses, and take a bottle of Teacher's upstairs.

The sleeping porch is cool, and they settle into the wicker chairs with the bar between them. Paige looks around. "This is a pleasant room. White wicker is such welcoming furniture. It takes me back to long afternoons reading the Jalna books. Did you ever read them?"

"I never even heard of them."

"They were great for a fourteen-year-old. Real grown-ups with sex, too."

Ward smiles and looks around the porch. She picks up some photographs on the table. "You know, I can't remember your ever talking about your father."

"For good reason. He was never around when I was growing up. He showed up the spring of my senior year in high school and told my mother that he wanted to send me to college."

61

"Did he?"

"Well, no. Mama thought and thought about accepting money from him. My grandmother was sure the whole thing was a ruse, but Mama kept thinking that he had changed. She finally called him and said that we would be pleased if he could give me the money. Do you know what he said?"

"No."

"He said that we must have misunderstood. He lived on a small income, and he didn't have that kind of money."

"So your grandmother was right?"

"As always. She said that she would sell some rental property, and she did."

They look toward the door when they hear a noise. Paige goes to the door. "Are you all right, Aunt Lotte?"

The light goes off in the bathroom, and a shadow goes down the hall and then closes a door. Paige returns to Ward. "She's in her silent period now, 'just drinking and thinking' as she says. She'll come out later when the level of alcohol gets just right."

"Has she always drunk like this?"

"I don't know. I only knew her until her second divorce. She had married her art professor her sophomore year at Georgia, and my grandmother had high hopes. My grandmother cut her off and barred her from the house after the divorce.

"What did she do then?"

"She went to Paris and tried to be a painter. We'd get cards now and again. Then she announced that she was married to a French artist. Years went by, and she appeared one day at the door with a strange man, someone from Alabama she'd met on the plane. She married him later, she said."

"What a story."

"Oh, that's no story at all, just a few facts. By the way, her first marriage was to Mrs. Jenkin's brother. They were just out of high school."

"She could write a book."

"Don't think she hasn't considered it. But she always says that other southern writers use her material. She really has it in for Pat Conroy. 'My father would make Santini sound like Uriah Heep,' she told me once."

"Well, she certainly can talk a good game."

Down the hall music begins. Paige and Ward stop talking and listen.

"This is her pitiful stage. 'I'll Be Seeing You.'"

"Wasn't she a bit young for war music?"

"Oh, no. She and Mama went to every movie, and my grandfather was overseas. She told me once that if you can't cry to 'I'll Be Seeing You' the tear ducts don't work."

62

"Do you think she'll care about us and our new life together?"

"I don't know. I do know that my grandmother would have had a hissy-fit. But the funny thing is that her sister Emma had a Boston marriage for years and years. I don't think anyone in the family ever understood the arrangement. She was just Emma's friend, Miss Norville."

"What did they do?"

"They taught music in a girls' college among other things."

Ward laughs. "Did Lotte like Miss Norville?"

"I don't think she saw her enough to have an opinion. People in those days just didn't think about women that way."

Ward mixes another drink and notices that Paige has her eyes closed. She is still holding her drink, but she seems asleep. Ward wonders how this weekend will end. Is it important that Lotte know? In her condition she might not remember anything they tell her anyway. She leans over Paige and takes her glass. Paige mumbles and sinks farther into the pillow.

The music stops, and Ward hears Lotte coming down the hall. She stands up and goes to the door. Lotte is carefully walking toward her.

"How are you, Lotte?"

"Just fine. I'm off to the kitchen for a refill. Care to join me?" Her letters are carefully formed, the words slowly delivered.

"Maybe later. Paige is napping."

"Well, carry on, Miss Ward, carry on." She goes down the darkened stairs, right leg down, left leg following, then right again.

Ward listens and thinks that she will never allow herself to live like this. She looks down the dark stairwell. She could turn on the lights, but they might frighten Lotte. Maybe she likes the dark.

She finds a bookcase in the hall, turns on a reading lamp, and begins to examine the titles: George Eliot, August Evans, Susan Warner, some history books, a few philosophy books, and some over-sized art books. The kind of books that her parents had before they moved to Boca. When she was young, she thought that a bus arrived when you were sixty-five and took you to Florida. As she grew older, she realized that in her neighborhood the idea was not so fanciful.

She pulls out *Macaria*. Probably Augusta Evans will come up at the conference. Paige has mentioned some interest in her. The nineteenth century woman writer has never interested Ward.

She wanders back to the sleeping porch. Paige is snoring now. Will she ever get used to her tendency to nod off and snore? Sometimes Ward awakens at night. There's a kind of purr next to her. She mentioned it to Paige once, and ever after Paige asked, "Was I purring again?"

She notices that the ice needs replenishing. She takes the bucket down. As she enters the hall, she hears conversation in the kitchen. She stops.

Perhaps someone dropped by to see Lotte. There's an older woman with her. Maybe Mrs. Jenkins has come over. She looks into the kitchen and sees only Lotte, a drink in her hand.

"You thought you'd have her the way you had her mother, but you lost her the way you lost me. What about that, Miss Centy?"

An old, strained voice answers. "What do you know, Charlotte? You were never anything but a disappointment to me."

Lotte begins crying. Her hand falls on her chest. "I know I was, Mama." After a few minutes, she looks up and then around the kitchen.

"And to think my punishment is to live with you in this house."

"You should have died in that accident, not Norma. She was the good one. Even when you were little, you were the bad one." Lotte laughs, finishes her drink, goes into the living room, and turns on the stereo. "Dancing in the Dark" follows her onto the terrace.

Ward gets ice in the kitchen and walks over to the window to watch her. Lotte is dancing now, turning in wide swoops, her arms reaching up. Ward can hear her singing, her words loud and out-of-time with the music. Lotte's arms go down, and she begins pulling off her gown. The light next door has been turned off, and the kitchen is dark now, only the low lights on the terrace shining on Lotte's figure.

"What's going on down here? Let me turn on some light," Paige says.

"Well, I just came down for ice, and Lotte was talking to herself in the kitchen, and I waited for her to finish."

"Where is she now?"

Ward points toward the terrace.

"Oh, my God, she's naked!" Paige runs through the living room to the terrace. Ward follows her. "Aunt Lotte! Here, put on your gown!"

Lotte looks at them, "Who are you? And who is that other woman? Norma, you've come back. Mama will be glad."

"Let's get her upstairs, Ward. She'll be all right tomorrow. She needs sleep."

They help Lotte into bed. Paige sits with her. Ward waits for her on the sleeping porch.

Somehow she knows that Paige has never really been hers. She was just a long way from home. Tomorrow she will be going from one program to another, but Paige will be here with Lotte. She will be talking to Mrs. Jenkins, who will advise her.

Paige appears in the doorway. Ward looks at her. "Is everything all right now?"

"I didn't know. I didn't know. She's all I have. I have to help her." She looks at her watch. "It's not too late to talk with Mrs. Jenkins. I'll call her."

Ward dreads the long ride home. She will be alone again, back on the river.

Reconnection

Aunt Mabel looked into the fire as I brought out my pen and notebook. I knew I had to let her start in her own time. Sometimes she went on. Other times she went to something else. Sometimes she came back later. I learned from yesterday's interview. "Now that's Tish's fourth, isn't it?" I asked.

"I told her the other day that I hope this was the magic number. Of course, I thought the third one would be the one. I thought James Kirkland would do right by her. I was wrong." She looked at me carefully. "You don't look like one of us."

"I know," I touched my hair. She followed my hand.

"That ain't your color, is it, Janet?"

"No. I started turning gray when I was in my thirties, and I decided to color it. I tried to get a color close to my real hair. My mother used to kid me about my hair. Hers was like yours."

Aunt Mabel touched her hair, smoothing strands behind her ear.

"I've had this old red hair all my life. Of course, they's white you can see when I take it down. I used to wear it down. I used to wear it long, but when I growed up and married, I put it up. They's a lot of us redheads in our family. Both Tish and Starr Ann." She looked at me closely. "We ain't much kin, are we?"

"I know." I had always wondered if I belonged in this family. I hesitated. "I think our grandmothers were first cousins. Would that make us kissing kin or shirttail relatives?"

"We'll just call ourselves family. You know, I always tried to get Tish interested in family, but she said that all those cousins were like strangers to her. She had a hard enough time keeping up with her own family. You know, she's not going by Tish anymore. She's going to be Marian Kirkland from now on. Kirkland was her last husband's name. She never liked her name — Letitia Mae Thigpen — was happy to get shuck of it."

"Where did Marian come from?"

"That was my sister's name. The one who died in that crash over at Pilgram Crossing in 1958."

"Wasn't Tish's first husband killed in a car crash, too?"

"No, that was her second husband, Tommy Lee Horton. He wasn't but twenty-four years old. Her third, James Kirkland, just up and left her for his secretary, Crystal Jones. They live down in Knoxville now."

I began to fill up the pages of my little notebook, the one I found at a garage sale without paper. It took me forever to find Mead refills.

I've got a good supply now. I'm trying to get organized. I tell my friends that I want "She tried to get organized" on my tombstone, and they always laugh. Besides, they will say that I have a few years left to keep trying. One good friend told me that I was creative not disorganized. I like her a lot.

Aunt Mabel put another log on the fire and settled back in her rocker. She put her hands on the chair arms. "This old rocker has rocked a passel of children. I've had the rockers replaced several times." She rocked and then asked me if I had children.

"I've never married, Aunt Mabel, and never will, I guess."

"That may be a mercy. Of course, you could still have some children. Why, I heard on the news the other day that some woman had seven children by seven different men. That's something, ain't it? And to get that on the news. That's really something."

"You can get most anything on the news these days except news." I went back to the interview. "What about Tish's daughter? I mean Marian."

"I still call her Tish. As I said to her, 'That's who you are. You can't go making up a new name and becoming a new person anytime you take a notion to. Starr Ann was a sight growing up. Just as smart and sassy as Tish ever was. Now there's someone who lives up to her name. Starr Ann Crenshaw. Now that's a mouthful, but I always loved leaning out the door and yelling, 'Starr Ann Crenshaw! Time for supper!' She'd hear that and come running from I don't know where and give me a big neck hug."

"Now where is she?"

"Somewhere up in Kentucky. She has a new job this year. I have the address somewhere. Tish always said Starr Ann would have a different life from hers. Melvin Crenshaw is her daddy in name only. You know, they split up right after the baby was born, and he took off where I don't know. Tish worked two jobs all those years to send her to college. Now Starr Ann is an English professor. I guess she's a lot like you."

I had never heard that story. Rather amazing, I thought, but there was a talent for storytelling that escaped now and again from the genes. I had heard that from my mother. She had that talent, but she never wrote the stories. I guess it's up to me.

I had not seen Aunt Mabel since I was a teenager. One summer my mother took me on a trip to see relatives. She introduced me to Aunt Mabel. "She's not really your aunt, but a cousin. We always called her 'Aunt' because she was an older cousin. Just a sign of respect, I guess."

We ate well and listened intently on that trip. My mother was afraid I would never know my roots. Usually she kept quiet about her roots to keep from embarrassing my father, who grew up thinking that his ancestors were special because they were on the Mayflower. One day my mother told him that hers were at Jamestown. I never knew if that were true, but that little factoid silenced my father, and he went back to writing the novel that he never finished.

Aunt Mabel wanted to know as much about me as I did about her and her family. "Now what about your folks?"

"My mother and father are both gone now. My brother Don lives in London. He's a BBC correspondent, and I'm still teaching in a college in Connecticut, getting ready to retire."

She looked interested but sad at the same time. "Your mama was something. She could out dance any of us. They's many a time I told her to stay with me rather than face your grandmother at 3 a.m. All our folks came and went, playing music and dancing, and no one thought about the time. But your grandmother was a town girl, and we only embarrassed her."

Aunt Mabel was right. My grandmother used to say to my mother: "That's your father's family — nothing but white trash living on the edge of a dime. I wanted more for you."

She sent my mother to boarding school for two years of high school and then on to college. My mother met my father at a newspaper conference when she was editor of her college newspaper, and the rest is history as they say. My grandmother could die then, satisfied that nurture had triumphed over nature.

"Now remember Starr Ann's name — that Starr is two r's. She's got the last name of my own mother, God rest her soul. She could have been a saint. Maybe she was one. Anyway, she took care of Tish when I had to get a job. When Crawford died, I took over his school bus job. I knew that route like the back of my hand. There wasn't a house I didn't know up here on the mountain and down there in the hollers. Yes sir, I've always had a map mind. I knew where to turn and where to stop. Crawford always said I was better than him. He didn't grow up here. He had to learn it all. I grew up knowing the lay of the land and the faces of the people. I always got the news, too. I knew who moved down the road, who moved away, and who went to the cemetery."

"That's a talent. I've never been good with directions. I remember that Erma Bombeck once said that wherever she was facing was north. I'm in her camp."

"You said your brother was in London. I think he must be lucky. Starr Ann went to London last year and sent me a card from the Tower of London. She saw the jewels there."

"I've been to London several times, but I've never seen the Tower."

"You ought to go. I told Starr to see it all for me and tell me about it. She's good that-a-way. I don't go nowhere much — just to the doctor over at Elizabethton, and that's not too often if I can help it."

"You look good. I assume you're in good health."

"Listen, Janet, anytime my feet hit the floor and I can get to the stove to make coffee, I'm grateful. The Lord don't seem to want me yet." She began to smile. "That reminds me. There was an old lady, Miss Clementine Sawyer, who lived down the road. She just kept living on and on, and she used to say, 'The Lord's set the table, but he ain't invited me yet. Maybe I should start saying that."

"I think you should, Aunt Mabel."

"You know, Miss Clementine would have been a good woman for you to interview. She was a honey, a real honey. Lived to ninety-six, she did."

"I'm sorry I can't include her."

"Maybe I'll make ninety-six. Who knows?"

"Just how old are you now, Aunt Mabel?"

"Ninety-two last July. I'm getting on up there. Remember, I was the oldest in the family, and your mother came along much later in her family. She surprised your grandparents all right. Sure did. Nothing before or after."

"Aunt Mabel, I think you're a marvel. You look good. Your mind is sharper than mine. And I thank you for letting me visit you."

"When you called, it took me a minute to recollect whose girl you were, but then I hit on it. I'm grateful for the company. Besides, I like the idea of your book. Tell me some more about it, Janet."

"Well, as I told you yesterday, my friend Amanda and I are preparing a book of stories about older women. We already have a publisher. We interview the women and then write their stories."

"And you think I'm old enough?" We both laughed. "You look like your mama when you laugh. Your brown eyes kind of scrinch up and sparkle."

"You are the first person to notice that, Aunt Mabel." I began to shuffle through my notes. Last night I copied my notes to cards. I learned the hard way to use cards to plot my stories. That's what I do when the stories piece together like quilts. The best way I write is just to sit down and listen to the voices. I hope I can write Aunt Mabel's story this way.

I looked at the fire and thought of all the people who had watched fires in this old fireplace. "Who keeps you in wood, Aunt Mabel?"

"They's a boy down to the store who cuts wood for me. His daddy is kin to me somehow, and he's real good about calling and bringing up groceries. I told him I wanted some real grits the other day. He told me he didn't stock it, but he was going to Kroger's soon and he'd look for me. He'll get it. I don't doubt it."

I looked over my notes and wondered about Tish. "You know, Aunt Mabel, you haven't told me about Tish's new husband."

"Well, Janet, I saved the best for last. He's a preacher on the radio. Aaron Mobley is his name, and he has a singing group. Tish took up with the singers —the Bible Tones — about a year ago. She always had a good alto, better than me, and she can sight read anything. A friend of hers from work took her along to a rehearsal one week, and she just clicked with the group. Aaron was married before to a lady who went to jail for embezzling money at a car dealership. He didn't know a thing about it because he was on the road preaching. He divorced her and married Tish. They're happy as can be. 'Starting all over again, Mama,' she said, and I could tell she was glad of the chance. She's just about played all the roles now: the sweetheart, the wife, the mother, the widow, the grass widow, and the other woman. Now she wants to be a good wife with some security. She can sing, and he can preach. I'm hoping for better days to come."

"Tish has had quite a life, hasn't she?"

"It's the stuff of fiction as Starr Ann says. You'll leave her a little to write about, won't you?"

"There's always plenty to write about, Aunt Mabel. I need Starr Ann's address. I haven't ever seen her that I can remember."

"She would sure like to hear from you. She always wondered about you. I once told her we had a teacher in the family. Tish was listening, and she said, 'I didn't know we had a student in the family, let alone a teacher.' Starr Ann piped up then, I'm a student, Mama, a good one, too.'

"Yes, you are, baby. How could I forget?"

Tish left school in tenth grade. I don't think she was school material. Her daddy took it hard, but I told him then about the baby and he began to get over the school part. Tish has been a good mother, too. Maybe she'll be a good wife to a good husband now."

"You know, Aunt Mabel, I ought to be getting along. I want to be on the road early in the morning. I have a job waiting for me in a few days."

"I'm mighty proud you came. I sure do want a copy of that book. Here's Starr Ann's address. Be sure to write her. She needs to know her family."

As I drove down the mountain, I knew that I had more than notes for a story. My time with Aunt Mabel would probably be my last time. I wanted to tell someone. Maybe I would write Don. I knew I would write Starr Ann.

Taking Temperatures

Natalie looked around the room. Nothing seemed different from the times she and Janey used to lie on the twin beds and talk about their junior high problems. The house had those heavy, dark rooms that women novelists write about. Young girls with tyrannical fathers, mothers usually absent, sometimes a brother or two, and no future in sight characterized those rooms. At the Lewis house the father was gone, the daughter visited from out-of-town from time to time, and the mother and brother lived on with a little local help.

"Are you all right in there, Natalie?"

"I'm fine, Janey. I'm just looking around. Your mother has held on to it all, hasn't she?"

"Never a figurine falls that she doesn't know about it. Buddy threatens to rent one of those garbage trucks and back it up to the front door."

Janey came in with drinks and set them on the bedside table. Looking at Natalie, she smiled. "I can't tell you how much we love having you here. We have all been looking forward to your visit."

"It's wonderful to be here. How long has it been? Four or five years? Except for you and your family, I don't have any connections here."

"You always have those in the cemetery, Natalie. Mother thinks that anyone who has relatives out there should visit them as much as the living ones, perhaps more."

"I might get along with them better."

They laughed and raised their glasses.

"Just like old times, Janey. When did we start drinking?"

"Probably a little bit after Buddy and his friends started. Maybe sophomore year."

"Now here we are two old divorced ladies hunkering down a little."

A car turned into the driveway. "That's Mother. Driving faster than usual. I expect her to take out the boxwoods at any time. Buddy and I will have to give her a Miss Daisy speech one of these days. I just hope she can hold it together as long as possible. People know her car and just pull over when they can to let her pass."

"Janey! Janey!"

"In here, Mother."

"I thought I'd never get home. I had to stop for gas. I went to that Starvin' Marvin out on the highway. I had to pump my own gas. First,

71

the gas wouldn't come out. I tried and tried. Then I had to go in. I took the gas cover with me. You remember that time I drove off and left it at the pump? Then the woman— Karen it said on her blouse— asked me how much I wanted. I told her twenty dollars' worth. You know, I don't know why people complain about gas prices. I just get twenty dollars' worth every time." She noticed Natalie and turned to her. "What a sweetheart to come to see us."

"I'm so happy to be here, Mrs. Lewis."

Janey took her mother's hand and told her that she shouldn't pump her own gas. "Besides, Buddy always fills your car on Thursday. Every Thursday."

"He didn't do it this week. He forgot."

"He does it on Thursday, Mother. Today is Wednesday."

"Today isn't Thursday?"

"No, Mother. Natalie came today— Wednesday. You remember I kept telling you Wednesday. Come on over here and sit down with us."

Mrs. Lewis sat on the loveseat, her over-sized pocketbook on her lap. She looked like a visitor in her own house.

"Put that pocketbook down, Mother. Buddy and I call her Queen Elizabeth. Have you ever noticed the Queen's pocketbook? She's always carrying it with her. Got all her jewels in it, I guess."

"Janey's always kidding me about my pocketbook. Did she tell you about the time— when was it, Janey? Last fall, I think. Someone cut the screen in the kitchen in her condo and took her pocketbook right off the floor, where she'd dropped it."

"Oh, Mother. That could happen to anyone. Not just in Atlanta."

"Not if you hold on to your pocketbook. Even when I'm sleeping, I don't let it go. I put it between my pillows."

"When Mother goes to sleep, she looks like she's planted in the cemetery with her pocketbook as her marker."

"What are you and Natalie having? Scotch? I'll take some, too. Too much excitement today for an old lady."

Janey brought refills and a fresh one. "Here's to Ladies Day!"

"That's what Janey calls my DAR meetings."

For a few seconds no one spoke, and then all three began and stopped.

"You go on, Mrs. Lewis," Natalie said, laughing with Janey. "Tell us about your meeting."

"Not much different. Fewer members every year. Mrs. Jones died last month. She was ninety." She hesitated and then looked at Natalie and Janey. "I don't know why you and Janey never had any interest in your ancestors. You both qualify. All the tracing has been done— several times over, in fact."

"We like our ancestors, Mother. It's the DAR we don't like."

Mrs. Lewis ignored the comment. She looked at Natalie. "You been out to the cemetery yet?"

"Not yet, Mother. Natalie and I will drive out sometime before she leaves. Maybe we'll take some pictures."

"Look at your Aunt Bessie's stone. Buddy said it was tilting last time he was out. We can get Mr. Morrill to fix it if it needs it."

"Don't worry about it, Mother. Buddy will take care of it."

"Oh, that Buddy. He's no better than any of them. I tell him things over and over, and he just keeps going. He's just like he always was. Just oblivious."

Natalie looked at Janey, who was looking at her glass. "Is Buddy still teaching the honors English at the high school, Mrs. Lewis?"

"You know Buddy, Natalie. He likes his routine. He goes to school, teaches some. I think he's got a bright class or two. I don't think he can tell the difference. He comes home, sits out there on the back porch, cleans his guns, and knocks over some bourbon glasses. He puts them beside his chair, gets up, and kicks them over. He says that it's all accidents. I don't know what to do with him." She looked up at the stained glass window and sighed.

"Mother, Buddy is forty years old. You aren't going to do anything with him at this stage."

The clock struck. Mrs. Lewis looked toward the hall. "What time is it?"

"Five o'clock or thereabouts. That clock is always thereabouts the real time, we always say. You worried about dinner? Natalie is taking us out."

"Oh, no, we'll take her out."

"We've already decided. Natalie wants to feel like an honest woman after all our times of taking her out." She smiled at Natalie.

"Besides, there's a limit to the amount of money she can spend at Shoney's. We're not talking about an elegant restaurant in Atlanta."

"Did you come through Atlanta, Natalie?"

"Oh, yes. The hardest part of my trip from New York."

"You remember Miss Addie Sue Randall?" Natalie nodded. "She went up there to do Christmas shopping and couldn't get out on the right road home. She finally flagged down a cab driver and had him lead her out of town."

They laughed and Janey suggested that Natalie try that the next time she had problems. "I'm used to it," she said. "The traffic is always intimidating. I always stay on the main highway through town. People call 275 the biggest parking lot in Georgia."

"Is Buddy going to meet us at Shoney's?"

"No, Mother, he's going to a dinner meeting of the historical society." Mrs. Lewis began to rummage through her pocketbook. She found her cosmetic bag and dumped out several lipsticks and a compact and began fixing her face. She opened several lipsticks before she found the right shade. When she finished, she rummaged through her bag again and found a tissue to blot her lips. "There," she said, "all done. A beauty break."

"You look very nice, Mrs. Lewis."

"Thank you, Natalie. You asked about Buddy. I'll tell you what he's doing that really interests him. He has been taking pictures of some of our local homes. He's making a slide show and doing research. He's doing the program for September for the historical society. You should come back to see it."

"I wish I could, Mrs. Lewis. I don't know where I'll be by then."

"Imagine not knowing where you'll be. I never thought I'd be anywhere but right here. I am always here. Mrs. Eula May Powers. You remember her, don't you? She's always saying that she wants to look up her Scottish ancestors. Her father told her not to in case they wanted to borrow money. 'It won't bother me, Daddy, I don't have any to lend,' she told him."

"She's right about that, Mother. Teaching school here all her life gives her about enough money to take a trip to Augusta every month or so."

"Let me go to the powder room, girls, and I'll be ready to go." The phone rang.

Janey answered it and held it out for Natalie. "We're just going to Shoney's. We'll be here later. Sure, I'll look forward to seeing you, too."

"Buddy's feeling guilty that he's not around to entertain you. He'll make it up to you later. He'll tell you all about his meeting. I think there're more members in his group than in mother's."

Mrs. Lewis led them through the kitchen to the carport. Janey asked them, "Why don't we go in my car, ladies? I just had it cleaned before I left Atlanta. Not often does it look this good."

Natalie helped Mrs. Lewis into the front seat and settled in the back. As they drove through town, Janey and her mother talked about one place and then another. Mrs. Lewis noticed new roofs, old windows that needed replacing, gardens that were untended, and general disrepair, but she always had hopes that things would improve. Natalie stretched back, closed her eyes, and half-listened. She thought about Buddy.

His voice took her back to that afternoon twenty years ago when they left school early and started off to get married. "We have to get married, Natalie. You can't do this by yourself." As she thought about telling her mother that she was pregnant, anything, even a marriage to a high school senior, seemed easy. Now the whole thing seemed laughable. They had stopped on the way to South Carolina to get gas, and she had

74

gone to the restroom and discovered that her period had started. When she returned to the car, she told him to take her home. They drove for thirty miles before she could tell him why she'd changed her mind. They went off to college and soon afterwards broke up.

As they passed the bank, Mrs. Lewis asked about the temperature sign. "How do you change Fahrenheit to Centigrade? I don't remember how to do it."

"I don't remember from physics, Mrs. Lewis, and Janey never took physics. You're asking the wrong people."

"Why is it important to you, Mother?"

"I just want to know. That's all."

"Well, maybe Buddy knows, but I wouldn't bet on it. If he took physics, I'm sure he didn't study. None of his crowd did though a good number of them became engineers at Tech."

The waitress gave them a choice of seats. "Not many here tonight," said Mrs. Lewis. She looked around. "A number of people I don't know."

"Mother thinks she ought to know everyone in town. She forgets that the interstate brings strangers through town."

They ordered soup and salad and later coffee and strawberry shortcake.

"I'm sure there are no calories in any of this," Natalie said.

"Of course not. That's why the Shoney's crowd keeps coming back. Mother loves to come."

"They say it's the dressings that do you in. That's why I just use oil and vinegar," Mrs. Lewis said.

"Just as long as there are no calories in the strawberry shortcake," Natalie added.

"Natalie, you have never changed. When we were little, you always said that strawberry shortcake was your death test."

Mrs. Lewis looked at Janey. "What was yours, Janey? Barbecue, sweet potatoes, banana pudding? You always liked to eat when you were growing up. Now that you're on your own, you don't take care of yourself. Are you eating three good meals every day?"

"Oh, Mother, you'll be wanting to take my temperature pretty soon. Wait until I finish this coffee."

As they drove back to the house, Natalie felt that she had come home. Years ago, her mother remarried and moved to Florida. When she visited them, she thought she was in a foreign country. Here she found things old and familiar. It would be easy to come back. What would she do if she couldn't get a job at the local college? It wouldn't be hard to fall into the old ways. What about Buddy? She laughed to think of her ex-husband in this environment. One Sunday without the New York Times would kill him. He came with her once and told her that he had never been to such a bizarre place in his life. He thought of

75

his neighborhood in Brooklyn as the norm.

It was still light as they drove in. Natalie and Janey walked on each side of Mrs. Lewis. "Let's go in the front door, Mother. We ought to use it sometime. We ought to enjoy the front door. We're always going in and out of the back door."

"When did you begin gardening here, Mrs. Lewis?"

"Oh, my mother did a little work here in the 1920's, when they bought the house. I really got interested during the war when Mr. Lewis was in the navy. Working in the soil took my mind off the war. Buddy and Janey and the gardening have always taken up my time. The yard is pretty, isn't it?"

"Lovely, Mother."

"I always enjoy walking around your yard, Mrs. Lewis. There's always something to see."

As they entered the hall, the clock struck eight.

"I'll put on some coffee for us and put out drinks for later. You two go on into the living room," said Janey going into the kitchen.
Natalie picked up a knickknack on the side table. "What are these, Mrs. Lewis? I remember them, but I've forgotten what they're called."

"Those are hair receivers. My mother had a few, and I began to collect them."

"I remember now. Women used to put hair in them when they brushed their hair."

"That's right. You've probably seen some of the pictures made with hair."

"What a dreadful thought," Janey said as she brought in the coffee.

"Here, Mother, fix yours. You still take yours black, don't you, Natalie?"

"Black and strong. Sludge in the bottom."

"Remember when we got to college and started drinking coffee?"

Natalie laughed. "A major step in our maturity. I think we had drunk everything else but coffee."

"You been out to the cemetery yet?"

"Mother, I told you that we'd go before Natalie leaves, and I'll look for Aunt Bessie's stone. Don't worry about it."

"Good. I'll tell Buddy, not that he'll do anything. He's just oblivious."

"Did I hear my name?" Buddy came over to kiss his mother and then Natalie. "I'll pass on kissing you, Janey, until you do something nice for me."

"Are you hinting about your birthday again" Buddy smiled and winked.

Mrs. Lewis looked at Buddy. "You look flushed. Do you have a fever?"

"I always have a fever when Natalie comes, Mother."

76

"Would you like coffee, Buddy?"

"Why not, sister?"

"Buddy, I had to put in gas today. You forgot to do it."

"You know I put in gas on Thursdays. If you can't remember the rules, you'll just have to suffer."

"Now, Buddy, don't talk to Mother that way. She had to go through I don't know what all to get gas."

"It's all right, Buddy. I had a good time waiting to pay. I just looked at those magazines. You know, you can't find that kind of information anywhere else. I like the stories about alien babies and lost children and unusual situations. One magazine showed a little girl who had given a kidney to a chimp."

"Oh, Mother, you're a sight. Isn't she, Buddy?"

"Mother's capacity for trash is endless. I channel my genes in that regard to the historical society."

"How was your meeting tonight? I should have gone with you. I always learn something interesting when I do go." Mrs. Lewis knew how to ignore her children's comments about tabloid journalism.

"Fine. Good group. A lot of interest in buying some things from the old hotel to go to the historic building. I think we can get some business people in town to underwrite the fountain that used to be in the hotel lobby. Should look good in our lobby. You would enjoy seeing our new building, Natalie. It's the old depot."

"It sounds good. Maybe I can tomorrow when I wander around with Janey. We're going out to the cemetery."

"Buddy, do you know how to convert Fahrenheit to Centigrade?"

"What? Fahrenheit to Centigrade? What for? Don't the weather forecasters tell you how hot it's going to be? Fahrenheit sounds hotter anyway."

"I just want to know the formula."

"I think I learned it once in physics, but I forgot it after the test."

"I told them that you wouldn't know it, Buddy" Janey said. They laugh and looked at their mother. "You're always making us feel dumb with all your questions. I'm sure we're fairly educated people, but you always want to know things that we don't know."

Janey refilled the cups with coffee. She noticed that her mother had started writing on a piece of paper. She stopped writing, waited, sighed, and then left the room.

"Mother gets these little flurries of interest now and then, and the world stops turning until she gets the answers. You must get a lot of questions, Buddy, from day to day."

"You know it, sister."

"Natalie and I have been thinking about the old days, Buddy. When we started drinking with you and your friends."

"A not-so-golden past, Janey. You and Natalie were fairly protected when I think about it. Some of us boys are lucky to be alive."

"That may be true to a certain extent, especially that part about you boys. When I was talking with Natalie, I began thinking about the time the two of you ran off to get married and then came back."

Buddy looked at Natalie. "That was one of the highlights of my senior year. That and the football championship, of course."

"You're so crazy, Buddy. I remember that afternoon like it was yesterday," said Janey. She cut her eyes at Natalie, who was looking at Buddy. "I kept thinking about what would happen when time ticked on and you were not around for dinner and I'd have to lie to Mother. I was sitting there on the porch worrying about it all, and there you appeared in the driveway."

"In my red and white Chevy. Now that was a car. I remember you bolted off the porch, squealing 'Where's Natalie? Where's Natalie?' "

"Let me tell you where I was, said Natalie. "When Buddy let me out, I sneaked up to my room and then came back down to help with dinner. My mother never knew anything. What about your mother?"

"Oh, Mother was worried to death about Buddy. He went up to his room and didn't come down to dinner. She kept asking, 'Do you think he has a fever?' She was ready with her thermometer."

Buddy laughed. "She always is."

By that time they were laughing so hard that they began whispering. "Be quiet. Stop. Don't say anything else."

"It all goes back to that big pocketbook," Janey said. "I know that she's had different ones over the years, but they're all alike in my mind. We were once at a family reunion and someone needed some scissors. 'Just a minute,' she said. In a few seconds this murderous pair of scissors emerged from her bag. Later on, a little cousin seemed to be feverish. My aunt asked my mother to feel her forehead. 'He does feel feverish. Let me get my thermometer.' Back to the bag and out came the thermometer."

"It's a family joke. Janey and I sit around with her and mention things we need: pens, paper, tape, vitamins, anything at all, and she goes searching through her pocketbook."

Mrs. Lewis appeared from the hall. She was smiling. "I have it now."

"Have what, Mother?" Janey asked.

"That formula for the conversion of Fahrenheit to Centigrade. It's C=5/9(F - 32). I almost had it. I just wasn't putting in the parentheses."

Janey and Natalie and Buddy stopped laughing and looked at her, and then they began laughing all over again. Mrs. Lewis took no notice.

"I called that nice Fred Mobley. You remember him, Natalie? He was in Buddy's class. He teaches physics at the college. He thought it was real smart of me to be wondering about it."

Janey laughed. "Unlike us, you mean. We think you're smart, too, Mother, but there's not a raging interest in this kind of information."

Buddy shook his head and whistled. "Isn't she a jim-dandy? All over America there're people who don't care a hoot about knowledge the way our mother does. Here's to you, Mother!"

"Thank you, son, and now if you young folks will excuse me, I'll just take a tot of whiskey and go off to bed. Thanks for the dinner, Natalie. I'll see you all in the morning."

"Goodnight, Mother," Janey and Buddy said together.

"Goodnight, Mrs. Lewis."

"It's hard to believe our mother. Buddy and I are always amazed."

"She is unusual, I must admit. I wonder if we'll be as interesting when we're her age."

"Probably not," Janey answered. "We haven't had so much leisure to let our minds develop in such exotic ways."

"I don't know about that," Buddy observed. 'Did you say that you two were going to the cemetery tomorrow?"

"We're going out to the old cemetery. You know, that one out by the Parker place. I forgot to tell you something, Buddy. Way back Natalie is related to us. Mother told me yesterday. She ran into someone who's been working on Natalie's great-grandmother's brother's family, and this woman told her that there was a connection with our Lewis line on our great-grandfather's mother's line. That tidbit made Mother's day."

"Well, why wouldn't it? That's great news. Natalie not only a favorite but a family favorite, a kissing cousin."

"I imagine almost everyone around here has some family connection," Natalie offered.

"Too bad, I'll be at school or I'd go with you to the cemetery."

"Another time, Buddy. Could I interest you in a drink to round out the evening?"

"Sure. We must drink to the old times."

Janey went to the kitchen for ice. Natalie and Buddy looked at each other.

"We've come a long way, Natalie. Ever think what might have happened?"

"Oh, we'd all be here having a nightcap. I would have gone to the historical society meeting with you, the DAR with your mother, and we'd have a couple of children at the University of Georgia."

"Would that have been so bad?"

"Maybe not."

"Here's the ice, Buddy. You may fix the drinks."

He filled the glasses and then held up his own for a toast. "To what might have been!"

"To what might have been!" Janey echoed.

"To what almost was," Natalie added.

She and Janey told Buddy goodnight and headed for their room, the same room that they had once used for sleep-overs. They began laughing as they closed the door and looked around.

"Just think. We can smoke and drink here now without sneaking," Janey said.

"No fun then."

They began changing their clothes, and the room didn't seem large enough. Neither one was orderly and neat, and they had given up hope. Janey looked around. "Our mothers would be disappointed to learn that we never outgrew our teenage housekeeping."

Natalie gathered up her clothes and stuffed them into a plastic bag. "They probably knew that we'd never change. They never set a very good example anyway. Besides, we had maids when we were growing up."

"Good point." Janey took some extra pillows and threw them on the beds. "Just like old times. You know, you look happy tonight."

"I don't know. It's easy to nestle in here for a few days. I need a little time. Just thinking about getting a new job scares me. I'm doing another one-year appointment. You know, the sabbatical-maternity substitute. After I left Dan, I thought that finishing my doctorate would take care of me, but it hasn't worked out that way. I may never get a regular job."

"Remember that drama course we took? Remember how Nora kept thinking something wonderful would happen?"

"I hope I have a better future than Nora. Ibsen is not comforting."

"I know how you feel in a way. I do have a permanent job if I want it. Museum work is interesting, but I don't have enough time for my own work."

"It's always money, isn't it?"

"Always. About ready?"

"Sure, Janey. Turn off the lights."

"Don't you ever think about coming back, Natalie?"

"Of course, I do, but what would I do? I doubt there's anything here for me."

"Maybe Buddy would know some people. I'll ask him."

"What about you?"

"Sure. I used to think I had to be in a city. Now that I have a reputation, I could work here and just take a batch of paintings to the galleries now and again."

"Your mother and Buddy would love to have you back."

"I know. You, too. You know it."

"Too bad we weren't born rich."

"I know. I always thought that." Natalie answered very softly. She felt sleepy, and they could talk a lot more tomorrow.

The next morning they went out into the county, left the paved road, and started toward the river. The cemetery was just beyond a little community consisting of a three-story house, a store, and several barns and sheds. They were weathered, long abandoned by a family that no longer lived in the area. The cemetery was well kept.

"Mr. Morrill does a good job out here."

"Who is Mr. Morrill?"

"I think he is an old boyfriend that Mother encourages now and again. He lives across the field there in that big old house. His parents died a few years ago, and he came back here to claim his inheritance and retire."

They wandered about, reading off names, remembering a few connections.

"Where is your aunt's grave?"

"Over here. The stone looks fine. We'll have to tell Mother right away or she'll never stop worrying."

They walked back toward the car and pulled themselves up to sit on the wall, their legs dangling. "Bringing in the sheaves, bringing in the sheaves," Janey sang, and Natalie joined her. "We shall come rejoicing, bringing in the sheaves."

"Did you ever wonder, Natalie, what sheaves were?"

"Something flat. You could stack them up like Christmas presents. I'm not sure what they are now."

"Me either. What about 'Just a Closer Walk with Thee?' "

"Do you remember that blind man who used to sit in front of the court house and sing? People always gave him money."

"I do," Natalie answered. "Do you think he was really blind?"

"I don't know. Probably not."

Natalie began pulling sandspurs from her socks.

"Remember how we used to look forward to going to town on Saturday?

"Sure I do. It was the highlight of the week."

"What's it like now on Saturday?"

Janey sighed. "The stores close at noon, and people go off to the malls in other towns. Mother really hates it. She wonders what Daddy would say. He always did good business at the hardware store on Saturday afternoon." They sat and listened to the silence, unrelieved except for an occasional bird. Natalie pointed her Reeboks out and then gave Janey a little kick, glad that she was not alone.

The Long Drought

She hadn't planned to go to the concert, but she ran into Dexter at the grocery, and he told her to be sure to be there.

"It's going to be tonight from seven to nine, Mrs. Gates, right out here in the parking lot."

"I'll try, Dexter. I'll try."

"You do that now. Take care."

He was one of her best students, Class of '76. That was a good year, she though. Maybe the best year she ever taught. Teaching English was a crapshoot, she always said. Sometimes the chemistry was just right, and then sometimes nothing would work. She used to think that teaching classes was like taking a Viet-Cong village and then having to take it all over again the next day.

As she left the parking lot, she saw the crowd across the street waiting for the bus to the Fair. Last year she was there with Hazel waiting. They went year after year, two retired teachers on a lark. They had a regular route, starting with the art and photography and then arts and crafts and finally senior citizens and wildlife. Hazel usually won a prize in the senior section for her watercolors.

"You ought to take something in, Willa. You would do well. I just know it."

"Oh, I don't know. Maybe I will." But she knew she never would. Maybe if Hazel hadn't died, they could have taken their art together. They could have continued to follow their route around the Fair. Willa always liked the rabbits and chickens. That section took her back to her Georgia childhood.

She'd been thinking a lot about her early years lately. She didn't know why, but she had been thinking about her cousin Joyce, just a year younger. When they were growing up, they lived on adjoining farms, part of the original farm, settled in 1832. "Generation after generation running to seed," her grandfather used to say.

Last summer when Willa visited, Joyce said, "We're a lot alike: about the same age, always on a diet, and looking for the perfect pocketbook." When Will was leaving, Joyce said, "Now remember: if you ever need to come home, we can always go to the Mercy Home together."

Willa laughed at the thought of the two of them in rocking chairs on the front porch. Joyce really meant it, too, about her offer. She was always ready to help out family. She had twelve brothers and sisters, but Willa was a special cousin. Since she was an only child, she and Joyce were very close. She had wanted to fly to New York when Harvey died, but Will told her not to. She had friends to help, she told her. Then she had Hazel, who was more like a sister than a friend from school.

Harvey used to laugh and hand the phone to Willa when Joyce called. "It's Joyce from Georgia." He would tell her friends that Joyce was the only person who called her Willadene and made it eight syllables long.

Around four o'clock she began thinking about dinner—maybe a tomato sandwich and iced tea. She didn't enjoy cooking for one. Since Harvey died, she made few meals. She enjoyed hearing about Haze's weekends as she cooked for children and grandchildren. Often on Monday mornings Hazel would drop off leftovers for Willa. "Here's a few items you can could try," Hazel would say.

"You're always giving me food, and I never cook for you."

"Well, you used to, and Bob and I remember what good meals you made for us."

Willa ate her sandwich around five and watched Wolf Blitzer on CNN. She was so depressed about the news and the prospects of war with Iraq that she often turned to Home and Garden to watch "Befores and Afters" and "If Walls Could Talk." She would chuckle to think what the decorators would do to her apartment.

After Harvey died, she sold a lot of furniture, loaded boxes for the Thrift Shop, and moved into an apartment on Main Street. She could walk to the Post Office and the bank and the video store and the grocery. She had her car, but she didn't use it that much, maybe a trip to Auburn now and then. After three years she was still not used to living alone. She sometimes thought: I live a mean, little life here, waiting for an ex-student to recognize me and tell me I look the same. That comment always amused her. She could only think that she must have looked really bad in her forties if she looked the same now.

Maybe she would go to the concert. Dexter always sang songs from the fifties. Maybe she would see some people she knew.

A friend used to tell her: "Go to Wal-Mart. You always see someone you know there." Willa knew that was true, but she hated to go. I was funny about Wal-Mart: no matter where you shop in different parts of the country, there were the same people shopping with you. Last December she was walking through the Wal-Mart parking lot after getting some film developed when she saw a couple with a little boy, maybe three years old. The father yelled, "Shut up," and the mother yelled, "Get in the car." The boy saw her walking past them and yelled, "Hey, look at that old woman." Wearing a black coat and black hat, she knew she looked old, but she didn't need a three-year-old boy to yell it out in a Wal-Mart parking lot.

Willa found a folding chair, an afghan, and her pocketbook and started out for the grocery store. As she walked, she saw neighbors on their way. They waved at each other. Willa thought, I have some waving acquaintances, no friends.

The parking lot was marked off with yellow ribbons. A few young people were running a concession stand. There were cars and trucks and motorcycles, and people kept drifting in from the lot and the street. She found a place in the middle of the front of the bandstand. Young children seemed to be everywhere—with young parents, grandparents, teenagers in charge of babies and toddlers. One young woman had very small triplets—little blondes who walked quickly behind her to get popcorn. After she bought popcorn, the little girls walked single-file behind her to get to their places: the mother and three little ducklings, each carrying a box of popcorn. Willa could imagine the work it took to care for them all day.

Willa had no children. She had pictured herself as a mother and grandmother. In fact, when she married Harvey, she saw her teaching career ending as her family grew. But she kept teaching, and her children looked at her from the other side of her desk.

Dexter welcomed the crowd and introduced his guitarist. His first few numbers Willa recognized, and she appreciated his mentioning the artists and songwriters for some of them, though she had no real ear for music and less for titles and lyrics.

The cashier at the grocery went out on the pavement with a man in a Hawaiian shirt and began dancing. He was excited to hear the fifties music, and he did a few steps over and over. She had a few more steps, which she did with the same enthusiasm she showed at the cash register—a frozen face and automatic movements. Probably in their sixties, she thought. There was a woman in front of Willa who took pictures of them and wanted to dance, but her husband was not encouraging.

In high school Willa and Joyce in high school went to dances together. They were both football cheerleaders, and theirs was a winning team. After the games there were dances, and they had steady boyfriends on the team. The girls wore the boys' big class rings on chains around their necks.

When high school ended, Willa went to a teachers college, and Joyce went to work in a doctor's office and married her boyfriend at Christmas. He was working then at his father's hardware store. He didn't get a football scholarship, and his grades weren't good. His father wouldn't send him to college to party. "Clark is not classroom material," he said, and Clark agreed. Besides, he had Joyce at home, and he wanted to stay.

Willa didn't find Harvey until she was in graduate school, and she sometimes wondered what would have happened to her if she had stayed home. Her old boyfriend sold insurance, and his wife stayed at home with their three children. Would Willa have been happier with three children and quilting and canning and Sunday dinners out after church?

The music caught Willa and took her back to the Hillsboro Diner, where she and Harvey used to go after studying in the library. Who was the singer? Billy Grammer? Or was that a student's name? Some of the lines she remembered from two songs, but she confused them. "I've played around this old town too long. . . .winter's coming on . . .oh, lonesome me." She hummed the songs, but somehow, they were one song, and she knew the feeling.

Maybe she was like the cashier: she knew the steps, but she had no life to her. She couldn't be like the others in the crowd. They were parts to a quilt; their lives were intertwined; their relationships were timeless; they had memories of each other; they had family secrets. To Willa, they were acting in a small-town movie.

She had acted in the same movie. Joyce sent her the hometown newspaper, a weekly that included social events, school news, real estate, obituaries, and crime and she read it, looking for news of her cousins and their children and grandchildren. She could take her folding chair and be part of them, listening to cousins of all stripes call her Aunt Willadene.

On the front page in the summer she had seen in block print a call for prayer:

> Praying for rain. A county-wide prayer
> meeting for rain will be held 7:30pm,
> Thursday, June 20, at the Jenkins County
> Agriculture Center. Local citizens as
> well as community leaders are urged to attend.

If she had stayed, she could have been a community leader at the prayer meeting. Looking around her, she realized that people were gathering their chairs and coats and blankets and calling their children. Dexter was thanking people for coming and then introducing and original song written in response to 9/11. The title was "Changes," and maybe she would remember it as she made arrangements to sell some more furniture and drop off more clothes and call Joyce.

86

The Ladies of Columbia

She had the front room in the house—the only bedroom on the ground floor. It was planned that way because Mrs. Rose was an invalid, who had lived with her daughter for twenty years. She lay in a hospital bed, her white hair spread against the white sheets. She was always beautifully composed as if a photographer were coming in from the hallway in a matter of minutes.

I was just one of the little children from the neighborhood, always tagging along after her three granddaughters. Because my grandmother went to school at Ward-Belmont with her, she was always glad that my mother and I visited her. In those days women took afternoon naps and visited in the neighborhood afterwards. I was almost one of the grandchildren as we crowded around her bed as she talked with us and patted our heads. After a certain time though, I could tell that Carla, Nora, and even little Nannie, who was named for her grandmother, dreaded her room because it was the scene of report card inspections, interrogations about lapses in behavior, and viewing of clothes. The girls began to take as little notice of her and her pronouncements as they did of their own mother, who stood alongside them at the foot of the bed, her hair growing white and wispy.

Sometimes I thought that Mrs. Handley looked like Mrs. Rose's tired sister. "A model daughter," people would say, and she would smile and thank them. "I do my best," she'd say. Mr. Handley had long ago given over the house to the women folk, and he only asked for peace and quiet when he came home from his grocery store.

Mrs. Rose interested me. I wondered how anyone could take to her bed and stay there. My grandmother told me that she had an aunt who did that because her father married a woman of whom she disapproved of. Mrs. Rose seemed so romantic to me, especially when my grandmother told me that her husband had been killed before her only child was born. He was a career army man who had gone to San Juan for what the newspapers called that "splendid little war." I couldn't even remember World War I. When my own father was killed in World War II, we talked less and less about wars.

"You should have seen Mrs. Rose at Ward-Belmont," my grandmother would say when I asked about her. "She was Nannie Alexander in those days, and we were all jealous of her and proud of her at the same time. When she married the son of one of the big Nashville families, we were as pleased as we could be. That was something for a girl from

Fayetteville."

"Was she really pretty then?"

"Of course, she was, child. We were all pretty then." Grandmother smiled at her little joke. "I guess the big thing was her ability to appear beautiful. She could get things from people just by batting her lashes. When Stephen Rose began to notice her, she told Jim how much she liked roses, and then he began to send them to her. Sometimes she would laugh about him and his roses, but she didn't hesitate to marry him."

"I still don't see why she'd just go to bed though." About this time my grandmother would be preoccupied with her embroidery and ask me to get her scissors. Sometimes when I came back from looking, she'd say she had found them in the chair cushion. She and my mother would exchange a look, and I'd usually know that an end had come to our discussion about Mrs. Rose. I always wanted to ask more questions, but I knew there would be no answers.

Carla was the first to break away, I remember. I knew that she had boyfriends. We all saw them coming and going from the house. As far as I know, Mrs. Rose didn't see too many of them. It was difficult for her to deal with young people who didn't seem to have the proper respect for the elderly. In fact, the boys hardly ever went into the house. Carla would bring out lemonade and cookies to them on the rambling porch. As we played around in the yards, we could hear her laughter drifting across the lawns. Once I saw her and a boyfriend wedged in the chimney corner, and I thought that certainly he must be the real boyfriend. But it turned out that she ran off with a college boy who was a senior at Vanderbilt. Her family put a good face on it—all except Mrs. Rose, who was upset that her granddaughter would not marry in the proper way.

After Carla left, the house and the yard seemed quiet, but I noticed that the other two girls left on dates more frequently than Carla had. They seemed always to be getting in and out of cars in those days. When I think back to the family, I can't really remember their father's face even though we bought our groceries at his store every week. We would wait for him to help us with our order; he was very meticulous and eager to please. He and my mother used to exchange pleasantries as he placed the groceries on the counter. Sometimes she would order, and the delivery boy would pedal out with the groceries carefully arranged in the basket. Mother always asked Mr. Handley about Mrs. Rose, and he always said that she was fine. Nothing much changed from year to year.

The neighborhood was quiet one October morning when I was home with a cold. I was allowed to sit in the living room on a couch and read. I felt like a Victorian heroine with my afghan and a George Eliot

88

book. I looked up and saw people on the lawn next door. I called my mother, and we both went to the window.

"What do you think is happening?" I asked.

"I can't imagine who that older woman is with the cane and the suitcase," said my mother.

I didn't know either because of her hat and veil. We stayed in the window and saw a cab stop and the woman go into it. There was no goodbyes, but Mrs. Handley and the girls stood around the yard with Mary, the cook, talking a long time.

We sat back and looked at each other. My mother was the naturally curious type who had to know details of all neighborhood happenings. I could tell that her mind was working toward a solution when Mrs. Loomis, another neighbor, came hurriedly up to our porch.

"Did you hear?" Mrs. Loomis still had dirt on her hands from her roses. She wiped them on her apron as she talked. "She's left them. Can you imagine that after all these years?"

"Who?" My mother was as mystified as I was.

"Why, Mrs. Rose, of course."

"You mean that lady was Mrs. Rose?" My mother's face was disbelieving. "She has been in bed for twenty years now. How could she just get up and leave like that?"

"Oh, Mrs. Rose had her secrets. That lady has been moving around for a long time now. When I took her flowers last week, she told me that she has been walking around the house late at night for years. She said that she needed the exercise." Mrs. Loomis sat down with her dirty hands in her apron, her eyes bright and eager.

"Now, Mrs. Loomis, that is hard to believe. I'm sure that Mrs. Handley would have been glad to have her taking some exercise." Sometimes my mother thought Mrs. Loomis exaggerated stories that she told. "Think of all those doctor visits and those poor people waiting on her as if she were a queen."

"It's a sad business - a sad business, I tell you." Mrs. Loomis looked through the window and shook her head.

"Where will she go?" I was so taken up with the recital that I wanted to hear the ending.

"She's going back to her home in Fayetteville, and the movers are coming tomorrow." Mrs. Loomis knew the whole story.
My mother looked toward the house and shook her head. "All the furniture downstairs is Mrs. Rose's."

"I know. Mrs. Rose wanted her furniture well cared for, and she would never sell it. She told me that she used a pillowcase to dust it at night when she got up, especially the rosewood piano with the Jenny Lind picture over it."

"Poor Mrs. Handley. All those years of putting her mother first, ignoring her husband, and letting her girls get away from her." My mother gave me a significant look as if to warn me about gossip. In fact, she suggested that Mrs. Loomis have some tea and that I rest in my room upstairs.

Reluctantly I went up and came back to the stairwell very quietly. I could only hear a word or two, and then I heard the front door close. When I ran downstairs, they were going through the opening in the privet hedge to the Handley house. I watched them go in, but I never heard my mother say anything about the whole situation other than "Poor Mrs. Handley." I'm sure that she and my grandmother had long talks, but I never heard them.

For the rest of that year, I saw Mrs. Handley occasionally in the yard, and I would speak to her. I began to notice that her hair was more carefully done up, and she began to wear gloves in the garden. She and Mrs. Loomis began to talk back and forth over their roses, and my mother would sometimes join them. The girls began to bring their boyfriends to their house, and somehow we were happy to hear the voices on the porch again. Carla often came in the summers, bringing along her young children.

In fact, for all my high school years the neighborhood was "quietly happy" as my grandmother used to say. We played tennis at Mrs. Laramie's courts on the hill or rode horses at the farm a couple of miles down our road. We began to ride bicycles in a group. The voices were heard on my front porch, and I began to serve lemonade and cookies and then leave in the early evening and come home late.

The Handleys did have two proper weddings, and we went to both of them with Mrs. Loomis. Now when I think back, Nora and Nannie have faces that get mixed up in my recollections of the Handleys. Mrs. Handley somehow sticks with me though because she became more beautiful as the years went by. Her hair was white, and her skin was as white as her mother's. We began to notice that she didn't come outside as much anymore, and when she did it was to watch the gardener.

By the time I came home from Ward-Belmont, she was staying in the front room. My mother told me that she had taken to her bed. When we went to see her, she looked as ethereal as an illustration in an old novel. Mary was still cooking for her, and she was always glad to see us and take us to see Mrs. Handley. "Mrs. Handley could do with a little cheer," she would say when we brought over flowers and candy. Sometimes the neighborhood children would stand around her bed, and she would ask about their grades.

We never heard from Mrs. Rose except when my grandmother mentioned her, but she never came to see her daughter or inquired about her or the family. Mrs. Handley never mentioned her mother except in some oblique way about the importance of having a real mother.

As time went on, Mr. Handley became even more involved in his business. He had one of the first supermarkets in town, and he was pleased to have business increasing. He began to work late hours to accommodate the demand. When my mother shopped, she always asked about Mrs. Handley, and he would say that she was fine. The delivery boy still came out for a few old customers.

My mother and Mrs. Loomis still talked over the roses and cut them for Mrs. Handley's vases because she had the gardener take them out and put in lawn. "After all," she asked, "Why do I need roses when I have such good friends with roses?"

The Summit

"She's here, Lutrell. She's here." The woman holding the door was not anyone Claire knew. From the kitchen Lutrell came, wiping her hands with a towel.

"Well, it's about time you got here, Missy. We've been waiting hours for you."

"I told you that I couldn't be sure when I'd get here. It's a long drive. I'm sorry for the inconvenience." Claire began to feel herself shrink to that little girl who always tried to placate her mother, the little girl whose favorite words were "I'm sorry."

"Well, aren't you going to kiss me? What kind of daughter can't even kiss her own mother?"

Lutrell opened her arms, and Claire waded into the folds of a Hawaiian mumu. She stepped back after a minute, admiring her mother's dress. "I like your mumu."

"Honey, this is a float. Mumus went out a long time ago. Just look at Foy and me together. Aren't we a sight--two old women dressed for action?"

Claire looked at Foy and smiled. "I haven't been introduced yet."

"I'm Foy Mobley, Lutrell's very best friend. We met the day she moved in, and we've been together ever since. I live right next door."

"If it hadn't been for Foy, I would never have made it. Since I didn't have any family to help me, I had to rely on a stranger."

"Well, I wasn't a stranger long." She gave Lutrell a little poke and headed across the room. "We had to start without you, Claire, being as how you were so late."

Claire looked across the room to a well-appointed bar with rows of glasses covered with palm trees. At least her mother was not sneaking drinks in the bathroom or under a pecan tree after dark.

"What'll you have, Claire? Lutrell has just about everything. She always says, 'I may not be able to give a man everything he wants, but I can make him a good drink, and that's the truth, too."

"I'll get something in a few minutes."

"Freshen mine up, Foy. I'll see to the roast. That second bedroom is yours, Claire, if you want to put up your things."

Claire moved through the living room, which opened onto a balcony. Turning right, she opened the door to her room. The whole place looked like a lesser movie star. Everything seemed to be shrouded in beige. There was a mistiness about the place with overhead fans whirring in the late afternoon. As she washed her face, she knew that the next few days would be further complicated by the decor and order of the condo. Every time she put something down, she'd feel guilty if she could not hide it. As she looked around, she realized that she had seen similar places before — Ramada, Howard Johnson's— impersonal and blank. If her mother could see her apartment in New York, she would never stop talking about it. She would use it as ammunition for years to show that Claire had not profited from a strict upbringing. A mercy, Claire thought, something hidden and only guessed at. Lutrell might use it anyway.

She walked back into the kitchen, where Lutrell and Foy were setting the table and dishing up food.

"We've become a good team, the two of us," Lutrell said, her arms going around Foy.

"The gold dust twins, people call us. We just about live together now that this honey has come to town."

As Claire looked at them, she saw herself and Lutrell. "The gold dust twins," Lutrell used to call them. "You can't tell us from sisters. Of course, I have a bigger bust, but Claire may get one if she's lucky." As a ninth grader Claire could only smile and distance herself from the scene, shutting off the laughter from Lutrell's admirers.

Sitting down at the table, Claire looked at Foy and Lutrell and waited. They waited, too.

"Aren't you going to say the blessing, Claire?" Lutrell never failed to find the weakness. For a second Claire couldn't remember a prayer, but a little voice piped out "For these and all our other many blessings, we give Thee thanks. Amen." Thank you, grandmother, she thought.

"We're right religious down her in the South, Claire. Probably you folks in the North have forgotten your religion," Foy said, slicing the roast and covering the pieces with gravy.

"Not much for me, Foy," Claire said.

"Oh, come on now. You've had a long trip and you need your food."

Lutrell looked at Claire. "You have put on a few pounds, haven't you? I could tell when you came in. You ought to take care of yourself, Claire."

Foy gave her a small piece of meat, and Claire ignored her mother's comment.

They ate quickly. The food Claire remembered from her grandmother's table. Creamed potatoes, peas, Jello salad, rolls, and iced tea. Afterwards Claire offered to clean up.

"That's real nice, Claire, " Lutrell said. "We did spend a lot of time fixing this meal. A lot of your favorites, too. I've got some lemon pie for dessert, but we can have that later if you want it. Foy and I will take our tea out to the balcony and watch the boats for a while."

94

"We could give her a little help, Lutrell, so that she knows her way around."

"She'll find everything. It's all right there — dishwasher and sink. Be sure to wash off everything before you put them in the dishwasher and don't put in the pots and pans. Wash them in the sink and clean the bottoms of the Revereware."

Alone in the kitchen, Claire did feel at home. For years Lutrell and Garrett had left the table and gone to the front porch, taking the tea pitcher along. As she washed and dried, she could hear the hum of voices mingling with the sounds of the house and yard. As she remembered, there was no winter, only summer, and she was always standing in front of the sink washing. She could see Lutrell and Foy on the balcony, their heads nodding to each other, their mouths forming words in familiar rhythm. Lutrell would set up the theme, and Foy would repeat it and add to it and then give it back to Lutrell to rework. Claire remembered her nightly talks with her mother, the two of them sitting on the darkened porch, following this same format. This was Lutrell's way.

She had not expected Foy. Lutrell had never mentioned her in her infrequent letters. Claire had assumed that her mother had little social life in the new place. Her pleas for Claire to visit seemed urgent unless she read carefully. The illnesses never had a name; the financial problems were trivial; the time on her hands somehow went quickly. "I have this friend whose daughter came for three weeks," she told Claire and they spent time at the sauna and took the weight-watching classes, and gave parties. She keeps asking me when you're coming." Claire wondered if Lutrell had a friend with a daughter. She should ask Foy.

By the time Claire finished in the kitchen, Lutrell and Foy had made their plans to go down to the club. "You have to go with us, Claire. We've been telling everyone that you'll be here."

"I'm tired, Mother. I drove ten hours today. I haven't even brought in all my stuff from the car."

Lutrell looked at Foy. "Isn't that just like Claire, always saying no to her mother?"

"We can take her another night, Lutrell. It's just the same old people. They'll see her soon enough."

"No, I want her to go tonight. I promised some people to have her there."

Claire looked at her mother and knew that the trap had sprung. There was no way to escape. Now she began the twisting to check out the clamps. "I'm not dressed for a social event, Mother. I'm still grimy from the trip. Not what I'd call proper attire for the two of you. I'm not a Florida person with a lot of summery clothes."

"No one cares, Claire. I'll tell them you're just out of the car. Come on, now. I'll get my purse so that we'll have a little drinking money."

Lutrell and Foy ran through the routine of shutting off and locking up. A ritual for a trip to Europe, not a stroll to a club on the property, Claire thought. The broomstick snapped into the bottom of the slider. Lutrell sensed Claire's observation. "You've got to be on the lookout at all times. There was a break-in last month in this very complex — Rancho Mermosa."

"Better safe than sorry," Foy said. "There're always strangers in paradise as I always say."

At the club the music was 1940's, the lights were dim, and smoke covered the tables. Lutrell waved to several people and then found a table for five. "We could have visitors tonight, seeing you are here, Claire."

"That's right, Claire. Your mama is just so proud to show you off. It's not every day we get a Yankee intellectual. You're downright uncommon."

"Gin and tonics all around," Lutrell ordered. As they settled down to drinking, Dorsey's band grew louder and dancers drifted out.

"You ladies out for the evening?"

"Oh, there you are, Jimmy. My daughter Claire. Jimmy is a retired dentist from Bayonne. Sit down for a minute."

In the darkness his hair looked like a handkerchief spread over his forehead. Could it be real? Claire wondered, His teeth had that sparkle of the TV ads. A perfect character from a soap opera, she thought. He seemed to suit Lutrell.

"We're just so glad to have you visit, Claire. You know what they say, 'If you get sand in your shoes, you'll stay forever.' I know it happened to me. Fifteen years ago, I sold my practice and came down with Martha. When she passed on two years ago, I just stayed on. After all, here are my real friends." He looked at Lutrell and smiled.

Lutrell and Foy smiled, and Lutrell patted his hand. "I can't tell you how much Jimmy means to all of us, Claire. He's a real rock."

"Your mama and I need a strong man to lean on every now and then," Foy smiled at Jimmy.

Claire drank and wondered how long the club stayed open. Her mother and Foy would last to the end. She had no doubt of that. Jimmy danced with each of them and started again with Lutrell.

"They're a sweet couple, aren't they? We're all pulling for Lutrell. She needs a permanent man. God knows a lot of us do. You can say all you want, but a man is what you need. You ever thought of remarrying, Claire?"

"Not really. I'm busy enough as it is. I don't need some additional responsibilities."

"In my book a woman should just put aside her own interests to make things easy for her husband. After all, men run the world, and that's the way it should be."

"Well, that seems to be the way it is."

Jimmy and Lutrell dropped by the table to say that they were taking a walk along the marina. Foy ordered another round of drinks, and Claire made a few suggestions about leaving.

"Well, I guess no one else interesting is going to show up tonight. We might as well call it a night," Foy finally said.

By now Foy's eyes glittered, her legs were a little unsteady, and she leaned on Claire going out.

"Point me in the right direction, Foy."

"It's just down here a ways. I'm perfectly okay. You don't have to help me."

Claire kept a hand on her arm and moved slowly. She could hear a few voices down along the water. She wondered if Lutrell and Jimmy were beyond talking now.

Foy found her keys to open her door and then Lutrell's, thanked Claire, and moved into her kitchen, snapping lights on and off as she headed for the bedroom. Claire watched until all the lights were off. She'll probably wake up tomorrow in her clothes and wonder what happened tonight, Claire thought. She was glad that Foy kept both keys with her. At last she could settle in. She left the door open in case Lutrell had forgotten her keys.

Lutrell had forgotten her keys. She stood in the shower longer than usual, washing her hair, scrubbing her body. I wish I could rinse out my mind, she thought. She could hear low voices as she drifted to sleep. She came awake later to hear noises in the next room, whisperings and things knocked over. Lutrell had brought in the prize for the evening, she thought, as she turned over in her side and went back to sleep.

When she woke, it was eight o'clock. The condo was quiet. She dressed, headed for the kitchen, and made coffee. Her mother's door was closed. Claire preferred not to see Jimmy this morning. Maybe he left in the early hours. We'll see how discreet Lutrell is in her new life, she thought. This must be an MGM movie for Lutrell. No more sneaking around to do anything. No more apologizing for an old house. No more barriers to living the life she'd always wanted.

How thoughtful of Garrett to die in an automobile crash and leave her so much insurance. "I want your mother to be taken care of it I should die," he told Claire. She wondered if Garrett would approve of Lutrell's new life.

Garrett would not be a condo person. Lutrell knew too much about him, and he knew too much about her. What it takes for a new life is lack of knowledge about the past.

Claire wondered if Jimmy really had been a dentist. He could just as easily have sold cars or insurance in Altoona or Camden. She wondered what kind of past her mother had invented. The time would come when Claire would have to verify whatever interesting details her mother might drop. "Mere embellishments," she used to say about her lies. "Who wants to hear the bare facts?"

Claire found the paper, took her coffee to the balcony, and stretched out. What would the day bring forth? The gold dust twins with their hangovers might pull down their blinds today. She was trying to finish a story she had begun last month. It was slow, and she wondered if it might join the others in the file. She looked at her watch. Nine o'clock. It would be a long day.

"Anyone up?"

Claire moved to the front door. Foy had changed into shorts and a halter. Her hair was in curlers under a turban.

"I'm the only one. Want some coffee?"

"Sure. I thought we'd go down to the pool and get some sun. You look a little peaked. Those hard winters in New York just ruin your complexion anyway."

"I don't tan. I just burn. I'll have to cover up if I go out. Can't take a chance on sunburn."

"That's too bad, honey. I always say it don't matter what the doctors say about cancer 'cause I'm going to get a tan anyway. I just think a woman needs a tan to wear her clothes well. Your mama has a glorious tan. Too bad you didn't get her skin." Foy looked toward the closed door. "She get back all right last night?"

"I guess. I didn't see her, just heard her."

They sat, drinking coffee and looking down on the people below them. Grounds crews were out trimming and mowing. Joggers went by. A few boats took off. A couple came by on bicycles. The world of the condos.

"There's always something to see up here. Never a dull moment."

"I thought I'd take a book out on the lawn and read later."

"You can't do that, Claire."

"Why not?"

"It's against condo rules to be anywhere but in designated places— the pool, the club, the condos or walking or riding."

"You mean that if I bought a condo I couldn't sit down anywhere outside?"

"Just the balcony but not outside the condo. They don't want the grounds cluttered up with people and chairs and things. Makes it look neater for prospective buyers. I guess it's a little hard on the grandkids though. You can't even let them play around the carports. Against the rules."

"Suppose you break the rules?"

"Well, you have to go to the condo court. It meets every month to take up cases. You can be fined."

"Sounds great. The new life has a few restrictions, doesn't it?" Claire smiled and wondered how these conservatives could sign away their rights to take a chair onto the grass. Sounds a little more restrictive than wearing a motorcycle helmet or a seatbelt.

The door opened. They looked back toward Lutrell's room.

"Been soaring with the eagles again?" Foy laughed, but Lutrell was in no mood for conversation about Jimmy. "I came home early. Why, I was here before you and Claire came in. Jimmy had to drive into Fort Pierce for an early doctor's appointment, so we called it a night after a short walk."

Lutrell brought out coffee and glanced over the paper. "The summer sales have started. We shouldn't let the clothes get too picked over. What do you say, girls? Hit the stores this afternoon? I'm in the mood for a little trying on."

Your mama has dieted herself into a size eight now, and she's just dying to get into some sexy outfits. What size are you now, Claire?" Foy disked

"Probably a twelve now. I've thickened up some through the shoulders."

"Get your mama's diet, Claire. She really knows how to take it off and keep it off."

"I'm not good on diets. I'll take my chances with regular food." Lutrell looked at Claire. "You used to be a lot thinner, Claire. You're just letting yourself go. We'll fix a little salad here and then go to the mall. Do you have some cucumbers, Foy?"

"I'll go get one. Be right back."

"Mother, I think I'll stay here this afternoon—do a little reading and writing. You know I'm not much of a shopper."

"Now that Foy's gone I want to say something, Claire. You just look awful. You're overweight. Your hair is stringy, and your clothes are ragamuffins. To think that you would look like this at your age."

"I'm not you, Mother. I'm busy with other things. Besides, I don't have the money to spend on beauty treatments and clothes."

Foy came back in. "Only had one. Listen, I'll make the salad. You two do a little mother-and-daughter stuff. I always say, 'A girl only has one mother.'" Foy went into the kitchen and began to pull open trays and open cabinets. Lutrell's kitchen was just like hers, and she could whip up a meal in a few minutes.

"Well, Claire, I'm going to take you to a place where I buy a lot of my clothes. Doris works there. She's been down here about five years now and she just loves it. She used to be a telephone operator in Buffalo, and she got tired of the winters. She helps me a lot with my clothes, and I told her to be on the lookout for you because I knew you'd come down here looking like you always look."

"It's okay, mother. I don't really want any help. I can manage. I'm all right the way I am."

"How can you say that? You're divorced. You have no children. You have a job that comes and goes. You're not making any money writing. And most of all, I bet you've got no one in sight. Not a man on the horizon. Am I right?"

"As always." Claire got up with her cup and saucer.

"Don't leave. I'm not through."

Claire sat down, still holding the cup and saucer, hoping to make a run for the kitchen at a juncture in her mother's conversation.

"Now get this straight. You're going shopping. You're going to buy some clothes, and I won't take no for an answer. Now go get on something to wear to the mall. Put on a girdle if you have one. You need it."

Claire took the cup and saucer to the kitchen. Foy was about through.

"It's always good to have a little mother-and-daughter chat, I always say."

"By the way, Foy, do you have a daughter?"

"Not so lucky, honey. All three boys. Big bruisers, too. I call them macho men. Just like their father. Big as an ox and soft as a pussy cat. I miss him every day."

"Mother mentioned that a friend of hers here has a daughter who visited her for three weeks and did a lot of things with her. I thought she might be your daughter."

"No. I don't know of anyone like that here. You must be mistaken. A visitor for three weeks would really stand out around here. You must be mistaken."

Claire told her that she was going to change. She had guessed that the daughter did not exist anywhere except in Lutrell's imagination. A three-week visit filled with weight watching classes and poolside tanning. Too bad that daughter couldn't come to visit Lutrell.

After lunch Foy left to change, and Claire came back to clean up. Lutrell passed through to give Claire some instructions. "You won't need the dishwasher for these few dishes, Claire. Just use the bowl in the sink to put some water in. Then just rinse them under the faucet."

Claire followed instructions and then dried, cleaned off the counter, and took the garbage to the dumpster at the end of the building. She helped Lutrell prepare the condo before they left. In the car Claire wondered what Doris had picked out for her. Lutrell drove and chatted. She could have been a tourist guide. "Well, here we are. A few places left. Listen, Claire, Doris has such good taste. Living in a big city like Buffalo gives a person such advantages in clothes."

As Claire followed Lutrell and Foy, she imagined clothes covered with bows and sequins. Just the things for the old USO club at the condo. Lutrell draped her arm around Claire and told her confidentially, "You have such potential. I always tell you that. Right?"

"Right."

"Of course, you do, Claire," Foy added. "Most assuredly. You are so lucky to have each other. I wish I had a daughter. I missed out on the buttons and bows."

When they arrived, Doris spotted them immediately. She stood with Lutrell and Foy, and Claire could only think of the Andrews Sisters. Doris kissed them and gave Claire a hug.

"A daughter of Lutrell's is like my own flesh and blood. I've been thinking for days just what kinds of things you might like for her, Lutrell. Something dressy probably. Up there in a college in New York she's probably got a little sloppy just going to class and working in the library. Is that right, Claire?"

"Right." Claire looked at the three of them and thought that the cauldron was missing. There was no escape, no hope of alleviation. No matter how obscene the outfit they would love it and insist that she buy it. Perhaps her mother would buy it for her. That idea was not strong. Lutrell never threw money at other people.

Doris put her arm around Claire. "I've known your mom since she came to Florida. She's a pistol, I tell you. What a lot of energy and enthusiasm. She's a pretty little thing. I can't believe that you're her daughter. You must look like your father."

"I guess so." How many times had she been told that? All her life. She had a hard time remembering her father. She knew that she didn't look like her mother, but she never saw much resemblance between herself and her father. She didn't know his relatives. Perhaps there were some people in his family she resembled. An old question.

Sometimes Lutrell used to introduce her as Garrett's daughter, and Claire and Garrett would smile and let Lutrell spin her stories. Claire had to admit that her mother could tell good stories.

Doris was holding an outfit. "Here's what I had in mind, Lutrell. Something a little fancy. I know you want to show her off at the club." Claire's worst fears were more than realized. It was black with a straight skirt and a V neck.

"Of course, a little jewelry would brighten it up. You know, rhine-stones are making a comeback," Doris added, holding the dress against Claire. "It's a twelve. That's all right. Your mother said to add a size just in case."

"Try it on, Claire," Foy said. "We want to see it."

When, she came out, the three of them circled her, feeling here, pulling there. They thought the dress was perfect — just what she needed.

In the dressing room she checked the price— $90. Just what she

101

had left to get back. She didn't want to add to her credit card.

"Well, Claire, we'll take it, won't we?"

"I don't know, Mother. The price is more that I want to pay."

"That's not a bad price, Claire, for such quality. It's just a little black dress. Every girl needs one."

"I'm sure every girl could use a little black dress, but I'm not every girl. I don't go out much. I really don't need it. I really can't afford it."

"Nonsense." Lutrell looked a Doris and Foy. "She'll take it."

The matter was closed. Claire came back with the dress and followed Doris to the counter. She counted out the money and waited for the tissue paper and the box. Doris was smiling. "You're going to use this a lot, Claire. I'm glad I could help you out." Doris gave her arm a squeeze and moved over to Lutrell and Foy. "You have one sweet girl, Lutrell. You take care now. Love you."

"Love you, Doris," Lutrell answered and took Claire by the arm, the three of them now fully armed against the world.

"We're on the town tonight, girls," Foy said, doing a little dance step. "Now, Claire, it's our turn to shop. We've got you something. You can come along with us and help us decide. Claire knew that the next few hours would be the longest of her life. As a child she had watched and wandered and watched again while her mother shopped.

Later, she helped Lutrell and Foy carry their packages back to the car. Piled in among the boxes and bags, Claire closed her eyes and waited for the car to stop at the condo. This is not a new life, she thought, just an amplification of the old. Just as Foy predicted, they dressed in their new clothes and set out for the club.

"Well, here they are in all their splendor," Jimmy said as they arrived. "I've been waiting for you, Claire. Your mother said that she was going to buy you a new dress."

"And I did, too, Jimmy. Isn't she lovely? Of course, she doesn't look a bit like me, but she's still lovely even though she insists on having a career rather than getting herself a husband."

When Jimmy asked Claire to dance, she went out on the floor, wondering how much longer she could stay. When Jimmy got himself settled on her, she thought she was back in high school, dancing in such a way that the boy whispered, "Wait a minute. Don't leave just yet." They went back to the table.

"Just like her mother—a real sexpot." He gave Claire a kiss. "You only get one, honey. The rest are for Lutrell."

Foy wandered off to the bar, and Claire followed. "Could I have my mother's key? I want to turn in early."

"Sure, sweetie. I'll be around here for a while. There's usually a little bar action on Friday nights from the tourists. Lutrell will be out with Jimmy again. Take care now, Claire."

102

"Thanks." She took the key, waved to Lutrell and Jim on the dance floor, and left.

She had not unpacked much so packing was not hard. The black dress she hung in the closet. She changed into her driving clothes. While she was looking for some paper on the desk, her mother came in.

"I was worried about you, Claire. Come on back. Jimmy is waiting for us."

"I'm leaving tonight, Mother."

"Leaving? You just got here."

"I know, but I have to get back for summer school. I'm teaching first session."

"What's that compared to your mother?"

"Please, mother. I have to take care of myself."

Lutrell was mixing a gin and tonic. She turned back to Claire.

"I've tried. Lord knows I've tried, but you're just like Garrett and his shiftless bunch."

"What? What are you saying?"

"You're like your father."

"You didn't say that. You said that I was like Garrett."

"Same difference."

Claire looked at her mother. The shadows gave Lutrell an eerie look. The jewelry gleamed. The mascara had run. The lipstick was smeared. The glass went to her lips and came back quickly to the counter. "You just don't have it, Claire. I can only do so much to help you. Tonight I dress you up and take you over to see my friends and you're not even cordial."

"Forget tonight. What about that other night? Are you telling me that Garrett knocked you up and you married someone else?"

"That's right, and then I married him after the war because I needed someone when I lost James. Garrett had this idea he'd go back to that beautician, but I showed her a thing or two. He came back to me because I knew how to have a good time. That was the best thing he ever did."

"And then die to let you go on? All those years you let me think he was just my step-father. All those years."

"Blow it off, Claire. What difference could it have made?"

"Hey, anybody home?" Jimmy came in and Lutrell went to him.

"Just a little misunderstanding, but it's all settled. Claire got a tele-phone call, and she has to leave soon than expected."

"That's too bad. I was just getting to know her. Now you come back real soon. Remember the sand in the shoes, honey. You'll never leave."

"Thanks, Jimmy." She looked at her mother and then left the room.

"Let's hurry back, Jimmy. Foy must be worried about us."

Two trips to the car, and Claire had everything in. She checked the closet again. The dress was by itself in the middle. Claire had slipped the price tag back on. It was cheap at that price.

Close Up

"Get the phone, honey. If it's for me, let them wait a minute. I'll be there."

She heard Mary Lou say hello, and then she heard her coming to the back of the house.

"It's for you, Mama."

"Who is it?"

"It's James, Mama. Long distance from Atlanta."

She followed Mary Lou to the front of the house. The long hall was dark. Brown figured wallpaper and a high ceiling gave it a gloomy aspect. The louvered door at the front was closed to keep out the late afternoon sun. Glass front bookcases lined the walls; they had originally held law books from her father, and now they had come down to her. She always felt pleased that she had spoken for them when no one else in the family wanted them. Her favorite books could now be under glass away from dust but targets for mildew. A book dealer had once told her that buying old books in the South was pointless for that reason. She still liked the idea of having her books away from the other books in the house. The phone was lying on a table at the bottom of the curved stairway in the entry. Wondering what James wanted or perhaps what he needed, she picked up the receiver and hesitated before speaking. There was no doubt that she would regret hearing his voice.

"James, it's good of you to call,"

"Mama, I had to call someone, and I knew you'd understand. Mabel has really left me this time, and I just don't know what to do."

"Now, James. Calm down. I can't believe that Mabel would just go and leave you. Did she leave a note?"

"Nothing, Mama. The car was gone when I came home from work. She's been saying she would, and now she has."

She didn't say anything, just looked at the books in the bookcase beside the phone. There was a set of Dickens in blue bindings. She really ought to begin reading them through again. A friend of hers wanted to read *The Iliad* through again and urged her to do so. Somehow wars and quarrels were not what she needed.

"Mama, are you still there?"

"I was just pondering, James. What do you think you'll do?"

"I guess just stay here tonight and wait for her. Maybe she'll come back."

"That's a good idea, James. You do that."

"Is everything all right with you, Mama?"

"Just fine, honey. Some of the girls are coming over to play Scrabble tonight, and Mary Lou is helping me make some chicken salad sandwiches for them. Do you think that would be nice for a hot summer evening?"

"Sounds good. Wish I had one right now. There doesn't seem to be much of anything in this house to eat. Guess I'll walk to the corner and pick up a few groceries."

"Well, now, let me know how things turn out. You know I'm always wanting to know how you are. Everything will turn out fine, you'll see. I know how these phone bills mount, so we'd better stop talking now. Take care of yourself, son."

"You, too, Mama,"

She heard the phone click and then the dial tone, and she placed it back in its cradle. She looked at the Dickens set again and tried to think which book she'd like to start with. Perhaps Copperfield was the one. She thought that James was something like his wife Dora; he just never could seem to manage. How she could ever have been the mother of such a man she didn't know? At least, he didn't live near her. She pulled out the book and took it with her to the kitchen.

"How are you coming?"

"Good, Mama. I'm ready to wrap them up and put them in the refrigerator. Can you manage them later by yourself?"

"No problem. Kate is coming over early to help me get things started. We'll manage real well. Are you going anywhere?"

"No'm. I'll be up in my room if you need me for anything." She walked to the door and turn back. "What did James want?"

"Oh, he was just a little lonely, I think. Life seems to press down on him sometimes."

"I guess so. It does on all of us sometimes." Mary Lou walked slowly up the hall and opened the door to look out on the late afternoon. She thought that she might go out on the porch and read for a little while. Perhaps the afternoon paper had been delivered. About this time, every afternoon, she usually went out to look at the plants and see if they needed watering. This had been her job since she was a little girl on this same porch. Nothing seemed to change, and she complained because it didn't.

Now she was grown, teaching school in town, but she was still the same a little girl living at home with her mother. At least James got away. She could not make the break. Sometimes people asked her why she didn't leave, and she told them about her mother needing help. That was not so. Her mother hardly needed anyone. She never even needed her husband. Nothing really changed in the house when he died. The fact was that she needed her mother, and she supposed James did, too.

Her mother was a dot around which circles of people drew themselves. Even those ladies playing Scrabble were drawn to her mother because she gave them reasons to think and feel. She left the doorway and climbed the stairs. Perhaps reading in bed with the fan blowing across her would be more relaxing than reading on the porch. At least the noise of the fan blurred the traffic out in the street. Their house was more and more in a commercial area each year that they lived in it.

The phone rang in the hall. She knew that her mother would answer it if she let it ring long enough. She could go to the extension in her mother's room, but it probably wasn't for her anyway.

"Hello," her mother said.

"Mama, it's James again. I had to call you to tell you that I'd made a mistake about Mabel. She was just out getting some groceries. She thought she would be back before I came in, but the traffic held her back."

"That's good, James. I'm glad you called. Give Mabel my love. Now take care of yourself."

"I'll try, Mama. You, too."

"Goodnight, James."

"Goodnight, Mama."

Maybe Pickwick would be better than Copperfield. She should exchange the books before she went upstairs. The bedside stand was filled with books that she was in the process of reading. Sometimes she tried to suggest things to Mary Lou to read, but she had given up. Each time she tried to recommend a book, Mary Lou told her that she didn't have time to read things that didn't relate to her school work. She never understood why books couldn't relate to school, but she supposed that Mary Lou was the type of person who would always explain her life away by saying that she didn't have the time. From all she could observe, that was all Mary Lou had a lot of time. In fact, she wished that she had less time so that she wouldn't be around the house so much.

The house was quiet now. The street was not so crowded with people going home. She looked across the street at the bank that had been built there. The house next to it was going for a parking lot. The woman who lived there was paid so much a month until she died, and then another house on the block would go. She wondered what would happen to her own house. Mary Lou didn't really care for it or its furnishings. James would never come back because there weren't any jobs here for him. She and her house had come through so much together that perhaps it would be wise that they die at the same time. Perhaps she would sell her house month by month like the one across the street. At least the idea was worth considering.

Time had become important to her lately. Last month she had an operation, and she could still remember it as a succession of long faces floating in and out of the hospital. Kate had become her official liaison with the public. As she expressed it, "Miss Agnes had the dearest little tumor removed." She enjoyed hearing this remark about the operation. Where else in this world would a malignancy appear benign and dear? She sometimes wondered how much longer she had. Actually, time was important to her only in relation to what she wanted to do. She would like to read the Dickens again. How long would it take her to finish the set if she read a chapter each night?

"Miss Agnes, are you back in the kitchen?"

"Come on back, Kate."

"I thought I'd come over as soon as I could to see if I could do anything."

"Mary Lou fixed up the sandwiches, and there's very little else to do. Why don't you have a little sherry with me while I set the table?"

"That sounds good. I could use a little something to perk me up."

Kate was in her middle sixties, and she was the kind of woman who came and went without notice. Except for her monthly circle at the church, their game of Scrabble was her big social event. Any other time she might have appeared as a spectator to life, but here in this kitchen she had some reality. Agnes was a hand mirror held to her face, and she smiled at the reflection she saw there.

"Is everyone coming tonight?"

"As far as I know, Florence and Katherine will be here. They went shopping this morning in Macon with their niece Louise, but they should be back now."

Kate watched her set the places, fold the napkins for the rings, and then adjust them so that they were evenly placed. There were Blue Willow dishes on the white tablecloth. Some pieces were old, and Kate liked to look at the old ones and compare them with the new ones. She thought that the birds were closer to kissing in the old ones, and she often mentioned this finding to Agnes.

"Everything looks nice, Miss Agnes. You always did know how to make a table look good. My mother used to say that it was not what you ate so much as how you ate that made all the difference to people. We used to use our best dishes for all our meals."

The phone rang. Agnes looked at the clock. It was five minutes until eight. Surely no one was backing out this late. She picked up the phone slowly, almost dreading to say hello. She wanted to postpone the inevitable moment.

"Hello."

"Mama, it's James again. I had to call you to tell you that I'm leaving home tonight."

"Oh, James, stop it. Why on earth are you leaving home?"

"Mabel and I had a terrible argument, and I just cannot stay here another night."

"I won't even try to talk you out of it. I would like to know where you are though. Will you call me in the morning so that I'll know where you are?"

"Sure, Mama. I'll call early before I go to work. I'm sorry I bothered you."

"It's no bother, James. It's just that I do worry about you. You're getting a little old to be acting this way. Just try to get hold of yourself and think things through. I'll be up early, so call me."

"All right, Mama. Goodnight."

She put down the phone slowly and looked down the hall. Kate was watching her from the kitchen, knowing that it was James. The door framed her, a small woman drinking sherry at the kitchen table. For a moment Agnes wondered who she was and what connection she had with her. Walking back to the kitchen, she took a place across from Kate and drank her sherry.

"Sometimes I wonder why I was so blessed with children."

"Don't say that, Miss Agnes. You've done a good job with your children. I can't think of two children who love their mother more than yours do."

"I suppose you're right, but there's no comfort in it."

The bell rang, and Agnes walked to the door, Kate trailing behind her in the dark hallway.

"Come on in, girls. We're waiting for you."

Florence led the way. Katherine stopped to pick up Leslie, a black short-haired cat that doted on being picked up and petted. "Were you waiting for me, Leslie? You know how much I love you, don't you?" Leslie was happy after being ignored all day.

As usual, Florence began talking right away. "We just had what I call an exquisite day in Macon. We had nothing really to buy, so we just walked around, had lunch, and spent a carefree afternoon."

"That's probably the best kind of shopping, Florence." Agnes led them into the living room, where Kate had already settled herself in her favorite chair, a blue Victorian lady's chair.

Katherine, still holding the cat, settled down and looked at Agnes. "This cat just gets more and more affectionate as she gets older—nothing at all like that calico you have."

"This one has a real need for people. The calico has been around here for eight years now, and she's hardly noticed me in all that time. She's the kind of cat that grew up autistic and vulnerable. She's unapproachable, always waiting for a blow that never comes."

"Oh, Agnes, you are waxing philosophical tonight," Katherine said. Leslie slipped away, and Katherine settled into the sofa, her hands reaching down to adjust her dress. It would ride up over her knees and show a satin slip with yellowed lace on the bottom. She always looked breathless and confused even in her more lucid moments. Sweets were her weakness, and she began to work on the bridge mix on the table. Agnes bought it especially for her, and it was agreed that she could eat it without fearing reprimands from her.

Agnes rose. "Why don't we go into the kitchen? Everything is all ready. I think that's the coolest part of the house with the door open. The house just doesn't cool off in the early evening." They followed Agnes.

Florence was the first to sit down. "What manner of good things have you planned for us, Agnes?'

"Nothing special, just chicken salad sandwiches, a tossed salad, and some tall glasses of iced tea. That's not much."

Kate pointed to the pickles. "How could you forget your very own pickles?"

Agnes smiled. She made pickles every year. She was the only family member who liked them, but she served them and gave them to friends. Now she was only planting cucumbers and tomatoes, and she canned both.

They ate slowly, watching each other and the food, hoping that no one would speak of diets and cholesterol. Florence ate with her head down near the plate, watching the food with great intensity. She moved the fork about and carefully picked out the green peppers in the salad. The others watched her. Katherine shook her head back and forth as a mother scolds her child.

Seeing the reprimand, Florence answered, "I can't help it, Katherine. I never did like green peppers even when I was a little girl."

"Don't mind her, Agnes. She's always been a little tetched about her eating habits."

"I usually remember and leave out the peppers, Florence. Sorry about that."

Kate stopped her fork mid-air, salad ready to drop on the table, and began to talk. "You're right, Katherine. Remember that time in the S&W when we had a basket of   rolls on the table? Florence opened one up to butter it and found a bug and just talked about it for the longest time."

Florence's eyes filled with tears, and she continued to eat with her head down. The table was quiet, and Agnes looked at the three of them and wondered what would happen to them if she died. Who could possibly assume the burdens of caring for the others?

They had not seen each other since last Monday night, when they met at Kate's and enjoyed tuna salad. Of course, Florence had eaten the same way as tonight; in fact, she ate every night as if the cook had plotted to poison her. Last week Agnes had won a magnificent game, depending on the word baroque to set her out in front of her opponents. She very often won the games, and she sometimes thought that they weren't any fun anymore if they ever were. Why she kept on playing she didn't know. When she thought of her children, she often added Kate, Florence, and Katherine to the list. Kate was a cousin of hers who never married, and Florence and Katherine were sisters who lived together after their husbands died. They were not related to her if this were any consolation at this point in time. Their socializing was predicated on the realization that no one enjoyed their company except the others in this room, and they would do nothing to upset the arrangement. Agnes thought about doing something, but she wouldn't really do anything to change the group.

They stacked the dishes in the sink and cleared away the table so that they could play. Agnes gave the cats the leftovers, and they settled down with their spoils and growled. Agnes made the coffee and plugged it in for later. There would be strawberry shortcake for dessert, and they usually stopped around nine-thirty for a break. Their general rule was to play one game after dessert and then go home.

Tonight was like so many other nights, and they held to their schedule. Agnes won again. Florence sighed and looked at the board. "Agnes, I don't know how you do it. I just feel so inadequate when you keep winning Monday after Monday."

"I'm just lucky in getting the right letters, Florence."

"Lucky, nothing," Kate rejoined. "When someone tells me that Kate Perkins is going to win a Scrabble game, I'll know that I have a new set of friends to play with. I still enjoy playing even if I never win." She smiled at her friends.

Katherine stood up and quickly sat down. "Oh, my foot is asleep. Did I ever tell you about the time I was in the college library, making eyes at a boy at another table? I jumped up with a reference book in my arms and just collapsed on the floor. I was so humiliated. He didn't even come over to help me up."

She looked around at her friends and waited for an answer that didn't come; they had made an answer a long time ago to that story, but she had forgotten. She got up slowly, and Agnes helped her. They began to move down the hall to the living room.

"I really mustn't sit down again, Agnes, but there is that candy dish. I'll put a few pieces in my pocket and be going."

"Just wait here, Katherine, and I'll bring the dish out to you." Agnes came back with the dish, and Katherine took a few. The dish was offered to the others, but they refused. As they stood in the hallway, a breeze came through, and the front of the house was much more pleasant than it had been. By eleven or eleven-thirty the entire house was cool unless there was a storm brewing.

"Hello in there." a voice called from the back door. "Oh, come in, Louise." Agnes went back to open the door for her.

Louise walked in, smiling at them. "I was afraid that our trip to Macon might have tired them out."

"Oh, no, they were just as chipper as ever."

"We may never win," Kate said. "But how can we complain with such good food and such pleasant company?"

They agreed to that, and Louise propelled them to the front door. They said goodbyes and promised to see each other soon. Standing in the door way, Agnes watched Louise carefully place them in the car as if they were fragile Christmas packages. The car doors closed three times, and then the motor started. Agnes waited there at the door until she could no longer hear the car. Except for the street light on the corner, the street was dark. She switched off the porch light. She had forgotten to leave it on for Louise, who remembered to go around to the back of the house.

It was too much trouble to clear away, so she turned off the lights, closing her eyes each time before she did so. Someone once told her to do that so she wouldn't be blinded by the dark. Actually, she could see rather well because of the hall light, which stayed on all night.

Passing Mary Lou's room, she hesitated but did not knock. She wondered if she had gone out for a sandwich or if she were on another one of her fasting diets. There was always a promise that she would lose some weight, but she wasn't strong enough to stick with it. What had there ever been to say to her? She had tried to make her daughter an intellectual companion, but the results were disappointing. How degrading to have her own daughter a mind plumber, which was her term for a nonintellectual teacher. What had always been essential for her was always peripheral for Mary Lou. Perhaps she had frightened her away. Perhaps she was never capable enough. She didn't know.

Once her daughter had told her that no matter how much she studied she would never equal her mother. It was probably a true evaluation, but why did she surrender to nothingness? Each year she was interested in less and less, and she complained about more and more. That was a curious way to talk of someone not yet fifty; that was the way to speak of old people. Perhaps that was her own problem; as she grew older, she was interested in more and more and only complained about people who weren't.

Closing her bedroom door and turning on the light, she began undressing for bed. The table beside the bed held several books in various stages of reading, and she noticed that she had indeed forgotten to bring the Dickens up to her room. She finally selected a book by Shirley Jackson, which had come out after her death. The cover said that Stanley Hyman had written the introduction. How nice, she thought, to have a husband who not only was an English teacher but also someone who believed in her writing.

Once she had felt an urge to write, and she had the time; but there was no one to share it with. When she wrote what she called poetry, people weaned off poetry by Longfellow and Whittier in school thought it was not really poetry. She looked over at a chest on the other wall. Inside the drawers were hundreds of poems waiting for her death to be discovered. Probably they would be consigned to flames because there was no one to care about them. She always came back to that old idea of caring.

There had been so few she had cared about. The ones she had cared most deeply for had not been related to her. Her son, her daughter, and her husband had always been non-people to her—weak, deferential, and totally uninteresting. She had tried with her husband, but she found that their ideas of conversational topics were far apart. He used to complain about the fact that she wouldn't talk to him, but she somehow could not respond to the things that he considered burning issues. He could talk for hours about the relative merits of bird dogs, horses, and bourbon, not necessarily in that order. As she watched his funeral, she kept thinking that dust to dust was too much, better to say nothing to nothing.

She was too tired to read. Turning off the light, she was soon asleep, dreaming of all kinds of people who talked of wild things. She dreamed of one of the few men she had ever cared about, and in the dream they were holding hands. Then she saw him moving across the room away from her. Looking down at her hand, she saw it holding a plastic hand instead of his, and she drew back quickly.

She woke up when the phone rang. Who would call at this hour? The clock indicated that it was 7:30.

"Mama, did I wake you?"

"Oh, no, James. I was awake. How are you this morning?"

"Fine, Mama. You told me to call, remember?"

"Yes, I remember, James. I hope you're pleased with the decision you made last night."

"I think I am."

"Where are you now, James?"

"I'm at home."

"At home? Why are you at home?"

"Well, I was planning to leave as I said, but Laurie and her family came down to spend the Fourth with us, and I couldn't just leave my own daughter."

"I understand, James. Try to get hold of yourself."

"Oh, I will, Mama. I'll try to get away next weekend if I can. I just can't stand it much longer."

"I'm trying to understand it all, and I'll think about it some more. Give the family my love."

"Thank you, Mama. Goodbye."

"Goodbye, James."

She put down the phone and looked at the cobwebs growing in the corners of the ceiling. One of these days they should be swept down. She needed a cup of coffee, to get going, as her friends said, and she thought she would make a list of all the things she wanted to do today.

In Ages Past

"Well, Sally, here we are after all these years."

"Here we are. It's been a long time, June," I answered, smiling at my grade school friend.

We were sitting in the library in her parents' home, the Queen Anne I'd always loved. She was much the same, still unwilling to attend our high school reunion. I was in town for the fiftieth and staying with Nell, whose mother taught me in fifth grade. It was a time to look back. "It seems like yesterday we were playing paper dolls on the porch," I said.

"I bet if I looked under the cushions of the wicker settee, I could probably find them," June said.

"Remember those bridal party dolls?"

"Sure I do. When we got tired of paper dolls, you'd read to me."

I looked at her and remembered the pigtails. We called her Margaret O'Brien then; now the hair, no longer brown, was cut short and needing dye.

"Now, Sally, don't look at me that way. I know I've let myself go." She began to laugh. "I always hated that expression when my mother used it about some neighbor."

"Probably Mrs. Mayson. I used to think she was at least eighty years old, but later I found out she was about fifty when she lived here."

I remembered Mrs. Mayson standing out on the sidewalk demanding to see our report cards before our parents saw them. We just handed them over and waited for her comments. I looked at June, trying to remember that little girl with pigtails, that little girl who wanted to know everything. I knew she wanted to know the gossip from the reunion. I didn't have to wait long.

"Well, Sally, how was the reunion?"

"You should have been there."

"Oh, no. I couldn't face people looking like this." She hesitated. "Did people talk about me?"

"I don't remember any real conversation about you, June— just a few who asked why you weren't there."

In high school June certainly was the topic of conversation— the first in our crowd to dye her hair, the first to own a car, the first girl to go all the way, and the first to have an abortion.

"You know, Sally, I've made a mess of my life. You know it. I was never smart and creative like you."

"Don't talk that way. You were always smart and creative. You had a good husband and a handsome son."

"You know I was never smart and creative. You were the one. You could have had Sam. You turned him down, and I was just around. I didn't deserve him."

"He was never serious about me, June. He used to say he didn't know what I was talking about after I read all those books."

"Believe what you want, but I knew the truth. He never said anything though." She paused. "It's been hard since he died. He just did everything for me."

June had always been a helpless kitten everyone wanted to take care of. Sam did take care of her, and she should miss him. I hesitated to ask about Lee, but I plunged on, hoping the news was good. Her son was like his mother: the subject of town gossip.

"Is Lee about to retire?"

"Oh, no, Sally. That last divorce really cleaned him out. He'll have to teach until the hearse pulls him away as he says."

"Do you like his new wife?"

"I don't see her enough to know. She was one of his students, and she seems to adore him."

That was a familiar story. I saw those little dramas time and again at my college. My favorite story is the one about the professor who left his wife and three children, married his student, and later left her and three children for someone he met at a Zen center. Lee left his first wife with no children. His second wife left him, taking her two children from a former marriage. Life may not be up to Lee's standards with his new wife even though she adores him. As they say, Lee is particular if not peculiar, living in the nineteenth century on the wrong side of the Big War.

"Did I tell you about the wedding?"

"I think you mentioned it in your Christmas letter. The rabbit motif?"

"Oh, yes, the rabbit motif. When Tiffany told me about her idea, I asked her for more clarification. That was a polite way to ask about it. "Say, what?" I wanted to ask. It was as tacky as you can imagine. The minister and her parents were so embarrassed, I think. I just wrote it off as something I would expect from the younger generation. Two ceramic rabbits by the altar, rabbits in a hutch at the reception, a rabbit cake, and rabbits all over the invitations and anywhere else she could think of. During the service when Tiffany read The Velveteen Rabbit. I wanted to hide under my pew. I just kept thinking that I hadn't brought Lee up that way. I don't know what happened to him."

"It sounds awful, June. Let's hope the marriage works out."

"Who knows? Lee might get worn out. Youth can be tiring and tiresome."

116

"Speaking of youth, I never thought you'd be wearing a T-shirt."

"Not just any T-shirt. This one is special— 'London, Paris, Rome, Cassville.'"

"I should get one before I leave. You know I read about one in a Siddons book, I think - 'Jesus is coming. Look busy.'"

"I love it, but I haven't seen it. Remember all those signs that used to be out on the highway. 'Jesus is coming,' they said. I think I believed them when I was young."

"We all did. The other day for some reason I thought about that Christmas Eve several of us went to the Catholic Church for a midnight mass and we saw the priest coming down the aisle."

June started laughing. "I remember his big feet in those heavy sandals. We all wanted to laugh, but we didn't."

I remembered, of course. What a scene. Seven girls kneeling and trying not to laugh. The kneeler was practically dancing on the floor.

We were always at some church service as I look back. Our friends were almost evenly divided between the Baptists and the Methodists. Catholics and Jews were beyond our understanding. June was a Baptist, and I was a Methodist. Once she told me to turn Baptist so I could be saved. "I wouldn't want to be in heaven without you," she said. I told her that I had to be with my parents in heaven and I was sorry I couldn't turn Baptist.

"I remember you planned the midnight mass experience for us, and we fell right in."

"I thought it would be exotic going to the Catholic Church and it was."

"It certainly was — especially for us Baptists. Methodists, too, I guess."

"You know, June, thinking back, I remembered all the times we were in church, but, I think, we spent more time thinking about the clothes we wore to church."

"We spent weeks planning our Easter outfits. What would we have done without Newman's Department Store? The irony was a Jewish store planning our Easter outfits."

"Remember that time we were at our college reunion going down in the elevator at the motel? You told me that Newman's was closing and a perfectly strange woman said, 'Oh, no, not Newman's,' and everyone on the elevator started laughing."

"I have to rely on you to remember things, Sally. I do remember that now. I can't believe how devoted we were to fashion."

I began laughing. "Or what Newman's told us was fashion. Remember Mrs. Stillman?"

"Oh, God, yes. No matter how you looked in an outfit, she'd say, 'Stunning, just stunning.'"

We laughed to think of ourselves in the fitting room with Mrs. Stillman, flitting back and forth with dresses on her arm. You could be in a size 18, and she'd just pull it back and tell you that it would be perfect with just a little alteration. If the buttons were popping on a size 6, she'd say, 'Just let it out a little and it will be perfect. Just perfect.'"

"Remember Mrs. Miller, Sally? She would come into the fitting room and say, 'June, take that dress off. It looks awful.'"

June suddenly looked at the teapot and cups. "Oh, Sally, what kind of hostess am I? I forgot the tea. A mouse could skate on it. Here try it."

"I'm sure it's all right, June. This is like old times. Your mother used to bring out tea for us on the porch."

"And gingersnaps. Don't forget the gingersnaps. I should have some today, but I don't bake anymore. I don't even go to the store anymore."

I wondered how often June left this room. She must use the daybed for sleeping. There were books on the floor, some open, some closed with bookmarks, and others crowded on shelves. Some shelves had VCR's, mostly British mysteries and masterpieces.

"Don't look at this room, Sally. I live back here. I always say to people, 'If you haven't seen me for several days, check my back room.' You remember this was the library when we were young. Now it's become the back room."

"Are you still collecting those Kathleen Norris books?"

"Oh, sure. I have a friend who stacks them up to take to the hospital. Maybe I should do that, too."

"Are you going to the hospital?"

"Not that I know of, but at our age, we have to be ready at any time. Those Norris books with the crazy plots and happy endings are just perfect hospital reading."

"You must enjoy this room."

"I do. I even have my sewing circle here. We meet every Monday. If you could stay over, you would really hear some stories. You'd be taking notes so fast your ballpoint would be on fire."

"What kind of sewing do you do?" Somehow I couldn't imagine June with a needle.

"I've learned to cross-stitch. Look over there on the wall over the desk. That is my Serenity Prayer."

"I see that a lot with alcoholics. Some of my friends have that stuck somewhere." I watched June closely, but she gave no hint of identification. Maybe the talk at the reunion was wrong. I remember going to see a friend in Charlottesville one spring. She had the prayer in her living room. Everywhere we went, she spoke to people she knew. I was puzzled. She hadn't lived there long. 'How do you know so many people in Charlottesville?' I asked. 'Oh, we're all in AA,' she said as if they were in a sorority."

"I've moved on from the Serenity Prayer though. Since Sam died, I've been working on 'Kind words can lift a heavy heart.'"

"That's a good thought, June. You know, I could get really depressed if I came back here to live. People recite a long litany of deaths, illnesses, divorces, and mental problems, and I've only seen those at the reunion-- except for you, of course."

"You just notice it because you're coming down from the North, where you don't know people that well. At least that's the way I see it. We hear things so much we just get used to them— except for Alzheimer's. I can't get used to it. After Mama's illness I keep looking for signs."

"Me, too. The other night I was watching the news and trying to think of the NBC anchor. Can you imagine? He's so familiar he seems like family. But wouldn't you know I went through the alphabet several times before I came up with Tom Brokaw?"

"You know, people are always asking me when I knew Mama had Alzheimer's, and I start this story about helping her with her groceries. That was back when Sam and I lived in Singing Woods. We got back to the house, and Mama started rustling around in her pocket book as we stood by the door. You know I never lock my door, but Mama always did. I asked her if she'd lost her key, and she said, 'I'm trying to get to my wallet.' She pulled out a one, rolled it up, and put it in the keyhole. "What are you doing?" I asked. 'Opening the door,' she said, 'but it's not working. I normally use a five-dollar bill.' It was so awful to think that my dear, sweet mother was totally bonkers."

"Oh, June, it's a good thing we can't see into the future. One of my best friends at my college lived for fifteen years after he was diagnosed. He was a brilliant professor in the English Department." I didn't want to talk about my parents, who died in a car accident when they were in their seventies. I hoped June would not bring it up. Her father committed suicide when she was in junior high, and we never talked about him.

"I used to think that just smart people got Alzheimer's, and I felt secure." She gave me time to smile. "But then I found out Mr. Jones had it."

"Mr. Jones? I don't remember him," Sally said.

"Oh, sure you do. He ran the furniture store."

"O.K. I do remember him. I went down once when I was visiting my mother. She wanted some new chairs for the dinette table. She had seen the ones she wanted in the show window. When I asked about them, he said, 'I'm not ordering them anymore. I can't keep them in stock.'"

"I don't think he had the merchandising gene," June said.

"No, his store failed, and his son Jimmy started selling satellite dishes. He's doing pretty well, I hear."

119

"What was that story I heard at the reunion about his marriage?"

"Oh, that. He and his wife Lorene had four boys— you remember— two sets of twins. One day he came home, and she told him she was leaving him to join an escort service at a hotel in Macon."

"I would think an item like that would make the rounds. What about his mother?"

"Oh, you can imagine her shame about Jimmy and Loreen and then Mr. Jones started failing. One day he backed out the car and ran over her while she was waiting for him to drive her to Wal-Mart."

"Did she die?"

"Oh, yes, and they had to put him out at the VA Hospital. Every now and again he tries to escape, and they call Jimmy."

"Every life a life of fiction, I always say."

"You ought to put us in your stories, Sally. You're far away, and we must seem exotic to you. You always had an eye for the exotic even when we were children. Speaking of children, I have to tell you about the little girl next door in your old house. There must be something in those walls to encourage her."

"What's her name?"

"Marnie. Her mother is Ashley, and her daddy is Al. He is a coach at the high school. Just the nicest couple. Well, anyway, Marnie came running in. 'Miss June, Miss June.' She calls me that. Her parents, too. Anyway, Marnie says,' Why does six hate seven?' I said I didn't know, and she said, 'Because seven, eight, nine.' Do you get it, Miss June? 'Seven, eight, nine.' I told her I did, and she just grinned."

"That sounds like real second grade humor."

"That's what she'll be in September, and I think she's going to be a real storyteller. Sometimes I wonder how much is real and how much is made up. There's a thin line there."

"Around here there's hardly a line at all."

"You're right, Sally. Marnie knows that already just as you did."

"Who knows? She could be a famous writer someday. I write, but fame has eluded me."

"You'll always be a famous writer to me. I still have that autograph book you signed. I got that little book for Christmas when we were nine, and I went running over to your house to ask you to sign it first. You didn't know what to write, and I told you to write how you wanted to be remembered. You wrote: 'Remember me as a famous writer,' and you signed it 'Sally Jones' and underneath you wrote 'Caroline Parker, my penname.' Later I filled up the book with little verses from my other friends. Not one person wanted to be remembered as something special. Maybe that said a lot about our generation."

"On that philosophical note, I have to move on."

"As Mama used to say, 'When the tea gets cold, and the paragraphs get short, it's time to go.' I don't agree. You should stay over. After the dinner tonight you could come over. You might have some reunion gossip for me."

"Who knows? I'll keep you informed. I'll write to you and send you some handouts."

"You're always so good about keeping in touch. Even though it's been years since you've visited, I feel like you're close by. I think little Marnie helps to keep you close."

"You've always been one of my biggest fans, June. I do appreciate your kind words. I guess I'll take off now. I want to check in with Nell to see if there are any plans for the afternoon."

"I forgot that you're staying with Nell. You should have stayed with me. I haven't seen Nell in a long time. They tell me her last facelift didn't work. You tell her hello for me. I just don't get out anymore."

I kissed June and held her. "Take care of yourself. Get out and see some people."

"I will, Sally, I will."

"I'll go now. I know the way out."

"If I weren't so comfortable in this rocking chair, I'd go out and hang on your car window to the end of the driveway for a few last words. As my Mama would always say to visitors, 'It you can't stay, tell me when you're coming back.'"

I kissed her again. "That's for your mother. She was always so good to me."

I went down the dark hall, the bright light from the porch guiding me out. I stopped by the car and looked at my old house. There were two little girls on the steps; one was reading to the other.

The Home Page

"Still looking for a job?" Marlene hangs up her mother's newly laundered sweat suits and smiles at her.

"Always looking, honey, always looking."

"Let's see. Do I remember it right? 'Companion on world cruise with handsome millionaire and large staff.'" They laugh.

Marlene memorized the ad from her childhood. Frances used to pretend to scan the want-ads for this position after her husband left her. She always told Marlene that she wouldn't take it unless she could go, too.

"No luck again?"

"No. I'm about to give up hope. Actually, I'm reading the obituaries."

Marlene settles into the visitor chair and watches her mother read. She tries to time her visits so that Frances can discuss the obituaries with her. Since she's been in the nursing home, she's missed out on several "funerals of note" as she describes them.

"Well, that rips it." Frances folds the paper, puts it into her lap, and looks at Marlene.

"What's that, Mama?"

Frances wheels herself to the window and looks out at the chickadees at the bird feeder. She slowly turns around to Marlene. "Do you have any scissors?"

"Maybe you do in your lower drawer." She leans over and pulls out a pair. "Here are your kindergarten scissors. What do you want them for?"

"I want to cut out an obituary."

"Anyone I know?"

"Someone I used to know in Augusta during the war. He's the last one."

"The last one?"

Frances cuts out the obituary and puts it into her shopping bag, which hangs on the arm of her wheelchair. "The last one who made love to me."

Marlene looks startled. "You've been keeping up with them?" She looks sly. "Were their very many of them, Mama?"

"For me to know and you to find out." Frances laughs.

"If you turn back to the window, you may see a man carrying a cross. I passed him a few miles back. He's taking confessions for Easter. Maybe you need to confess your sins."

"A man carrying a cross?"

"He's planning to be in Savanna by Sunday."

"He's carrying a cross?"

"Well, after a fashion. He has wheels on it. His son helps him, and his wife is following in a sport vehicle. She's got a cellular phone. Martha Downs told me about him last night."

"For a minute I thought you stopped to confess to him."

"No, not me. I didn't see anyone we know talking with him."

"Honey, the people we know can hardly get to the grocery store, let alone find a man with a cross on the highway!" She touches her hair and looks innocent.

"When is your appointment?"

"At three." She starts laughing. "I forgot to tell you. Angelique doesn't want to be called a beautician anymore. She an esthetician."

"My aren't we getting fancy! Esthetician. Why, I can hardly say it. Does she give you a bit of philosophy with the wash and set?"

"Not unless you count gossip as philosophy. Although she does manage to work in some philosophy after the gossip."

Marlene smiles. "Anything new since last week?"

"The only thing I can think of is that fire out at the Newton place. You remember the son died in his room?"

"Oh, yeah. He came in drunk, and a friend put him to bed with a lighted candle. I never took him for the candle type."

"No one else did either. There's a story there. Stay tuned for breaking news. They're not ruling out homicide."

"Really? Right here in River City. I'll have to tell John. He knew Hank when they went to Vacation Bible School that summer he stayed with you while I went to Milledgeville to finish my certification."

"Have you talked with him lately?"

"Last night, in fact. I think he's feeling a little sad now that he's graduating. He'd stay in college forever if he could."

"Does he have any plans?"

"He's all over the map — just knows he's not coming back home."

"What does Ernest say?"

"He told him all along that the small hardware is doomed. Besides, John didn't get the merchandising gene."

"He must take after you. Remember that Christmas you worked at Woolworth's? You came home every night complaining about standing on your feet and talking with customers."

"Do you remember that? I'll say. I think I told you that if I ever need money that badly I'll borrow it. Of course, it does sound an awful lot like teaching school, doesn't it?"

"Well, we ought to know."

Marlene looks at her mother. Even in her wheelchair, she has that glamour she always had. Dressed in a purple sweat suit, she wears her pearl earrings, an array of gold rings and bangle bracelets. She looks as if she's just visiting a friend. Marlene knows how much Frances wants out.

"Oh, before I forget it. I dropped off some Braswell's fig preserves at the kitchen."

"Thanks. I need little reminders of home."

"No problem. Now let's get serious. How is the therapy coming along?"

"I'm hoping to take a few steps soon. I want to. I really do."

"I know you do." She walks over to her and gives her a kiss. "And you will, too." She sits back down and spreads out her skirt."

"You look like those catalogs, Marlene."

"I guess that's a compliment. Long, paisley skirts with a T-shirt hanging out seem to hide a world of imperfections." She touches her hair, now growing out from years of red dye. She wonders what color it will finally be. Too bad she can't have her mother's white hair, so neatly captured in a bun. Marlene struggles with her wild curls every day and prays the weather stays dry. In the humid weather she calls herself Medusa. Frances always tells her she is lucky to have curls and reminds her of her Shirley Temple ringlets she had as a child.

"You going to let your hair go natural?"

"I guess so. God only knows what color or colors it may be."

"You've got your grandmother's hair—the Scottish side of the family. One of your father's better contributions. She still had some auburn hair when she died at ninety-three."

"Something to look forward to, I guess. By the way, the new Jan Karon book comes out in April."

"Good. I need a new one. I lent out the others to Carrie Lou's mother."

"That's nice of you. Is Carrie Lou doing well?"

"Just fine. She'll drop by in a little while."

Marlene looks at the flowers across the room. "Your arrangement is holding up well."

"Yellow mums and purple Siberians are always good. I've enjoyed them. Thank Ernest for me again."

"I'll bring you some of your daffodils when I come back Sunday. Your yard looks wonderful."

"Well, you know, I always try to put another hundred in every year."

There is a pause as if one is waiting for the other to say something important, but the moment passes. Then they both start at one time.

"You go ahead, Mama." Marlene seems relieved to give over the conversation.

125

"I was just going to tell you about Dorothy Brown. Did you hear about her?"

"No, did she have another accident?"

"Oh, yeah, she did. She was out in the country at night going to a church committee meeting. She got lost. The overhead light wasn't working so she got out to read directions by the headlight. The car rolled over on her foot. It was her left foot, so she drove herself to the emergency room."

"How old is she now?"

"About seventy-five. Younger than me."

"Well, that time she ran into the front of Bi-Lo? Shoppers were screaming, and she was looking around as if she were at the movie house. I hope you don't start scaring people and hitting buildings, Mama."

"If I do, just tackle me and take away the keys."

"I'll try." Marlene begins thinking about the time she'll be driving her mother everywhere. Then she wonders about the time in the future when she herself will need someone. A few weeks ago, she would not have been thinking this way, but now she'll be alone. She looks beyond her mother to the window, trying not to let her voice quaver. "It will be hard, I know."

"Did you go to Rutledge last week?"

"Rutledge?"

"You said you were going with Josie Applewhite."

Marlene comes back from her thoughts, pleased to have the conversation take another turn. "I'm getting to be one of those old ladies looking for the perfect teacup."

"Did you find it?"

"Probably not, but I found one I liked anyway. White with pansies and gold trim. I'll keep looking, of course."

"What's Josie doing these days?"

"She's on the internet now. I was surprised I could lure her away. She always hurries in to see if she has mail. It's just about all she does now except for church."

"A TV is enough for me."

"Are you sure you don't want one for your room?"

"Oh, no. I can wheel into the lounge. After supper we always watch *Jeopardy*. Last week the final question was Presidents' Birthplaces. We felt pretty good until a painting came up on screen— a side view of Grant Wood as we learned later. No one had ever seen the painting."

"Whose place was it?"

"Hoover's."

"I've never seen his house. Did anyone get it?"

"No." She looks at Marlene and waits. Will she tell me now? How long will she wait? Maybe she'll get around to it soon. I'll have to keep things going a while longer.

"I forgot to tell you, Marlene. Rosa Lewis dropped by. She wanted to know about the accident. She'd heard I'd turned over the car when I was changing a CD. I told her that was right. She said, 'What was the CD you were changing? You know how she is— always wanting to know the littlest thing. I told her it was Andy Griffith's hymns."

"Oh, Mama. You don't have that CD."

"I know. I thought she'd like that and spread it around. Besides, it gave us something to talk about. She used to watch that Mayberry show. She still watches reruns."

Marlene laughs. "What were you changing?"

"One of those Johnny Mathis CD's you gave me. 'Chances Are' is one of my favorites, you know."

"What's Rosa doing these days?"

"She's hip-deep in genealogy. She says she met some distant relative who has traced their family back to William the Conqueror."

"If I know her, she'll move the research on so that she connects with Mary and Jesus."

"Marlene, you're terrible. She's just an old woman looking for some importance in her life."

"Well, she can't depend on her relatives to give her any importance."

"She told me that Little Wayne just got out of boot camp. He's a changed boy now, she said."

"Let's hope so. I'm sure life in Millen was safer with him out of town." Marlene glances at the space under the bed and sees a box. "What's that under your bed?"

"It's a bee house. I want you to drop it by my place. Willie Parker brought it over. He heard my squash didn't do so well last summer."

"I heard something about mites taking out the bees."

"That's it. I thought I had bad seed. Now I feel better. I have to find a good place for it."

"We'll find a good place. Something for you to think about. You can tell me, and I'll put it up."

"Maybe I can put it up myself. I need things to look forward to."

"Sure you do."

For Marlene, today is like so many other days. The words float back and forth. Maybe she should have arranged for lunch out. She could have told her then. Somehow Shoney's didn't seem the right place. She looks at her watch. 12:00. Lunch will come in thirty minutes.

The door opens, and Carrie Lou sticks in her head. "Miss Frances, lunch is coming in about thirty minutes. You all right, Miss Marlene1?"

"I'm fine. Your family all right?"

"They're doing good."

"Did I hear that your grandparents' trailer burned?"

"That was last fall. They moved in with us." Shy and hesitant, she stands close to Frances.

"Is there something you want to tell me?"

"It's that paper, Miss Frances. I wonder if you'll look it over."

"Sure, Carrie Lou. I'll be happy to."

"Thanks so much. I do appreciate all you've done for me." She looks at Marlene. "Good to see you, ma'am. We're taking good care of Miss Frances for you." She closes the door.

"Marlene, she's such a sweet girl. Taking' classes at Swainsboro Tech and working here to make some money."

"It's nice that you can help her out."

"Good people ought to be encouraged. I've always said that."

"You've done a lot for people, Mama. You keep up with so many of your old students."

There were times that Marlene was jealous of her students. Now she's pleased that they remember her mother. Their children and grandchildren remember her, too.

"I keep up with a lot of people."

"Some might call that gossip, Mama."

"Oh, no, Marlene. That's news. There's a difference, you know. Now that story about the fire — that's gossip. We don't know what happened or why, so we speculate."

"I should have asked you if you knew any news then."

Frances laughs. "What's that Rosa Lewis used to say? 'I'm not going to tell you twice so listen the first time.'" They both laugh.

"Next time I'll just ask you what you know."

Frances searches Marlene's face. Will she ever get around to telling me? The time is not right yet. Maybe I can get her to talk if I tell her about a movie. "Did you see *Love Letters* on AMC this week?"

"No, but I saw it a long time ago. Joseph Cotton and Jennifer Jones. He writes these beautiful letters for a friend, and she marries the friend."

"It was so real to me. I thought about your father and me. People make big mistakes. Sometimes they are just not meant for each other. Sometimes they start off right, but they drift apart."

"You know, don't you, Mama?" Marlene feels relief, but she still has to tell her. "Ernest moved out last week to the camp, but he's looking for a house in Savannah."

"I'm so sorry, Marlene. Ernest seems like my own son. I feel bad that I may have contributed to your troubles. All that time looking after me, worrying about me."

"Don't think that. His girlfriend is young and independent— owns her own travel agency. What did you hear?"

"All I heard is there's someone else."

"Well, that someone else lives in Savannah. At least it's no one in town. I would hate it if she lived here."

"Does John know yet?"

"No, we thought we'd tell him this weekend. He has his vacation coming up. At least it's not at his wedding. Do you remember that story about Ted and Judy Jenkins? They told their daughter they were splitting up at her wedding. That really took the edge off the reception."

"I remember, and then they were back together a few months later. There's no accounting for people and what they'll do to their children."

Frances tries to think of some words of comfort for Marlene. All she can think of is "It's not the end of the world," a few words handed down for generations from mothers to daughters.

Marlene is crying now. She pulls a tissue from the box on the bed table. "You knew, and you didn't tell me. Here I am just agonizing, and you're just waiting like a plumped bird to hear it from my lips."

"Well, you know I don't like to repeat gossip. I thought I'd wait for you to tell me. Then it would be news."

"Oh, Mama, you're the limit." Marlene is laughing now and crying. "What would I do without you?"

Frances smiles. "Well, you have a lot of decisions to make. Maybe I can help."

"I know. I can get a condo, I suppose. Take a class. Get a computer."

"Oh, Marlene, that's what they all do. You can do the unexpected—stay in the old house, read Jan Karon books, eat Braswell's fig preserves, watch AMC, talk with your friends, and read the obituaries."

"That's what you do, Mama!"

Now Marlene is really laughing. "I guess I'm just a perfect candidate for the Woman Alone. I already know the lines."

"You were always good with memory work, Marlene. You don't need wheels on your cross. You can carry it."

"We're back to Easter, are we? We were talking so hard we must have missed the man with the cross."

"Maybe next year. Something for us to look forward to."

"I suppose so. Sunday John and I will be here for the service. So you want a hat?"

"Bring that picture hat with the roses. It's in the blue-striped box in the top of my closet."

"Sure thing. I'm going by to water the plants anyway and cut some daffodils. Anything else you need?"

"You can bring that new teacup you got in Rutledge."

"It's just a cup with pansies, Mama."

"You told me that, but I want to see it."

Holding On

She was reading a first novel. Did that mean it would be very good and she would want a second, which might never come or be a rehash of the first or might go off in another direction, the author trying so hard to keep people from saying, "She only had one story in her after all." A young girl, an artist, in Wales between the wars. Everyone knew which wars. It was a time of throwing up our heels and letting it rip. That's what her aunt Rose used to say when her sister wasn't around. Now Rose was gone, and her sister had her friends at the senior home. She was the reason her daughter had come home.

Her mother was reading the Bible with her friends and attending Bible trivia sessions. Maybe that's what will happen to me, she thought. I could find Jesus as I sit with my friends in an air-conditioned room, listening to a series of religious speakers coming in to share the gospel. She wondered if her mother really believed or she just wanted to be in the group. After Bobby died, her mother said she lost her faith. But maybe she had it back. She talked differently now about a lot of things. She discussed her hair and removing a mole on her face. "I know it's just cosmetic, but I'll be glad to pay. It would make all the difference." She wondered if she would care if she herself were ninety. "Good for her," her friends said.

That girl in Wales seemed to matter to her. That's what she wanted in a book now—someone to care about. She remembered reading books that never had a single person worth worrying about. Now she had a rule: Read fifty pages to test the waters; if it didn't interest her, close the book and pass it on. The library sale, the Salvation Army, a friend who killed time with words and had too many at home to care about fictional characters. She liked a good story— the kind you didn't want to end. Every now and then she pulled out Anne of Green Gables and reread it. She hadn't read it as a child, and now she wondered if a child could read it. Sometimes she had six or seven books beside her bed, just testing time, hoping for the right one.

She looked around the living room and wondered if this house were worth her time. "I want you to live in it while I'm away," her mother said. "You need a place now that you're retired. All those years in Buffalo. I can't believe you're here."

She couldn't believe it either. All those years of teaching, all those years of turning the ignition and hoping the car would pull out on a winter morning. Not a morning went by that she didn't wonder why she was living in an upstairs apartment in Buffalo. It was the kind of place that had the look of arts and crafts, but she never go involved with it.

She would watch the Home & Garden Channel and think, good for them. What a good idea. Why don't I want to spend my weekends looking for junk and spreading it out in my apartment? Her idea of a good project was to find a Victorian novel she didn't know and read all day. The fifty page test didn't apply to Anthony Trollope or Charlotte Younge. She could always keep going. She thought of her reading as opening drawers in old dressers and pulling out old clothes and family jewelry. Not expensive things but worth looking at. She could do that now. Her mother only took what she would need. Getting her to that point wasn't easy. She had to do something with all the other things. Always fearful that her mother would ask for one of the paisley shawls, she left them in the cedar chest. She knew that the thrift shops dealt in vintage clothes, but she couldn't get herself together enough to load up the plastic bags and drive them off.

Sometimes she thought her life as a teacher was like her father's. They went out each morning, she with her papers and lunch, he with the newspaper and his lunch box. Back at night, they started dropping their burdens in the kitchens. He picked up beer and pretzels. "Men drink," her mother said. "I hope you never start." As she looked back, she thought that alcohol got her through the winters in Buffalo. At least her father could fix a electrical problem; she never knew how many students she fixed.

That young girl in Wales would be about the same age as her mother. Did she become a real artist or did she marry a returning soldier and have several children and clear out the art supplies for a neighbor's son who needed them? "Better that he have them than leave them in the top of the closet." That's what her mother would have said. That would be the end of it. No one in her family had the talent or the time to make pictures.

One day last week she had read the obituaries as she usually did and found a woman who had died in her seventies. After the obligatory information, the only other information was that she played bingo every Thursday at St. Bridget's. Imagine sitting around after her death, her children trying to think of something to say about their mother and coming up with, "She played bingo every Thursday at St. Bridget's?"

What would be said of her? She had no children to write an obituary. When her father died, the obituary listed the church and his job as an electrician and then the survivors. "Not much to remember," her mother said. "That's the way life is." Maybe she would write her own. She ought to write her mother's or have her mother dictate it to her. What would her mother think? She'd go in and say, "Hi, Mother. Let's do your obituary." What would she say? "You'll be glad when I'm gone. I know you will." Be prepared, she told herself. Be ready. She could do it on Saturday.

She started off Saturdays with a one o'clock visit after her mother's exercise class. Maybe this Saturday. Then she went to the grocery. I need to make a grocery list. She looked through the kitchen window. Why don't I plant some tomatoes? Her mother used to plant twenty-four plants every year. Celebrity, Jet Star, Big Boy, and Roma. And can, Lord, could she can! She would push down those Romas with a spoon. "Keeps it thick'" she'd say. Maybe she could put that in the obituary. "Always planted twenty-four tomato plants and canned the Romas." Probably there were some jars still in the pantry, all cleaned and turned over with rings on them. Who wants canning jars? Does anyone still can? She had never canned. DelMonte does a good job, she thought Maybe she could write her obituary and personalize it with a reference to her love of Victorian novels. "She's one of the few who ever finished The Daisy Chain."

When she heard a noise at the front door, she started down the hall. There's the mail. Probably nothing personal. She was right— begging letters. Most of them were to her mother. A few were hers. Where had they found her name? A few contributions here and there and then the avalanche began and even multiplied. She put the mail in the basket on the window seat.

Her brother's World War II picture hung on the wall near the window. Her mother was so proud of Bobby. She said with great pride, "My only son." When he didn't return to Cedartown after the war, she spoke of him with reverence. He became more saint-like every year. She wondered what her brother would have become. Probably he would have worked with his father, but his mother had other plans. She was thinking of the church. She was the only one. Not even the nuns at the high school would have recommended him. Her father would smile at her mother and shake his head. "Your mother has always been a dreamer." She thought of her brother late at night throwing rocks at her window to wake her up. She would creep down the stairs at 2 a.m. and help him into his room. He was like the Welsh girl's brother in the book she was reading. That young girl waited up for her brother, too. Sometimes Bobby couldn't throw rocks. Someone else knew her window. His friends would carry him from the car to the porch, where she'd be waiting in that pink chenille robe she hated. Her mother told her it was practical and, besides, why would a young girl need anything else?

She laughed a little as she looked down at her violet chenille robe. Violet, now that was a Victorian word. She needed a summer robe, something light and loose. She didn't wear a robe much anyway. She always dressed in the morning— not like Aunt Rose, who used to begin dressing after supper for the long evenings. "Don't be like your Aunt

Rose," her mother would say. "You know what happens late at night in the back seat of cars." Rose began to tell people she was married to a sailor who had shipped out— someone she'd met in Charleston. Rose was always one for visiting a cousin in Charleston. "You should see us, little one, walking arm and arm down King Street. Sometimes we'd sing 'Pistol-Packing Mama' and dance a few steps on the way to meeting our boyfriends."

"Hush up, Rose. Don't tell her those stories. She'll grow up thinking that's what she should do." She never thought that. She never wanted anything to do with sailors. Besides, she never saw sailors in Cedartown. Only the Jones boy, and he didn't get home very often. They never saw the sailor Rose said she married. One year Rose didn't come home at all, and when she did, she looked really pale. Her sister was so good to her, trying all kinds of food she knew that Rose liked. Rose never talked about Charleston again.

As she was leaving for the senior home, the phone rang. "Yes, yes, I can come over. I was on my way anyway." She put down the phone. Maybe it's nothing, she thought. Maybe it's just her anemia. She's fainted before. The last time she was sitting beside her mother's bed when she opened her eyes. "Rose, is that you, Rose?" Maybe this time she would recognize her only daughter.

On the Stoop

Just look at this place. It's not what it was. I guess we all are not what we were. Certainly I'm not. I used to get out there and work and work after breakfast until lunch time and never even feel time passing.

There was one summer when I grew zinnias, cleomes, and cosmos together — all pinks and whites and purples I like those colors, you know. Denise, my daughter, put a stop to the flowers. She had Chuckie (that's what I still call my grandson) put down black plastic and woodchips around some hostas, and that's was it.

I remember when I was a child, my mother planted hollyhocks down by the barn. We were a farm family then. Sylvia and I came into town for school. When we lost the farm, we moved here to this very house. For a long time, I lived at home and worked at the hardware. I was a bookkeeper. Sylvia went away to teach.

My father used to say, "Sylvia's too plain to get a man. She's got to go to teachers' college. You'll do fine, Earline. You'll get a man." That was important then: get a man. Back then, nobody asked the children what they wanted to do.

I used to ask Denise, and she'd say, "Oh, Ma." Chuckie's no better. "Oh, Grandma," he'll say.

Denise had to get married. Just sixteen. She moved in with Clarence and me when Alan took off. I hear he's done well. His parents sent him on to college, and he has a good job at the bank over in Calhoun and a wife, who is a schoolteacher. He never sees Chuckie and getting any money from him is an ordeal. Denise just won't stay after him.

Denise had to leave early today for a doctor's appointment before she reports to Wal-Mart. She's been working there for a couple of years now in the restaurant. She works late, and Chuckie comes home from school and sees to me. I told them that I can see to myself, but they will nag and remind me of the time I walked downtown before Chuckie came home from the high school. Denise said, "We can't have you running off to town." I didn't run away. I just walked down to the drugstore. Denise is always carrying on like that.

What's the use? I always say. I'd like us to have dinner together, but Denise is at Wal-Mart's, and Chuckie stands over the sink eating a cheeseburger and drinking a Mountain Dew. When I was a girl, my mother gave out the new napkins on Sunday, and they were beside our plates all week. Denise forgets to put out paper ones.

Things just keep changing and not for the better either. It's like the poet says:

> *The Moving Finger writes; and having writ,*
> *Moves on: nor all your Piety nor Wit*
> *Shall lure it back to cancel half a line,*
> *Nor all your Tears wash out a word of it.*

Denise and I went to Emma Jenkins funeral a few weeks ago. She was our next door neighbor on the right side. A sweet girl, she was. Her son and his family came from North Carolina. There were two boys— not boys really, young men. They looked like handymen— blue jeans and dirty t-shirts. Emma would have died twice to see them. I made Chuckie promise me he'd wear a jacket to my funeral. Denise said, "If you behave yourself, I'll take off my Wal-Mart uniform and give you a good send-off.

Emma had a good send-off. She always liked funerals. She used to count the people at a service and compare the number to other services. Sometimes she'd say, "Now that was a good turn out." Denise referred to her as a "funeral junkie." Once Denise called her to tell her to sign her name to the book at the funeral home. Of course, she did that for lots of her friends. I wonder if the families ever knew. Probably they used to ask her, too.

I think a lot about dying these days— not just me but Sylvia. She's in an assisted living place, not far from here. Denise goes, over, but I don't. Sylvia never calls me. I always ask Denise how she's doing, and Denise will say, "About the same." Then I'll ask if Sylvia asked about me, and Denise will say, "Oh, sure." I know she doesn't. Why would she? She doesn't care. She never did. Oh, what's the use?

After Sylvia went away to teach, we only saw her on holidays and in the summers sometimes when she wasn't going to summer school. She had this friend, Nadine, who used to come home with her. A little too mannish for my taste, but then Sylvia always looked that way herself. A few years ago when Nadine died, you would have thought she was family. That's what I said to Sylvia. I guess I put my foot in it as they say. I'm glad she doesn't take it out on Denise. Every week, Denise drops off newspapers and magazines and checks on her clothes. Once Denise asked if she needed anything, and Sylvia said she needed some girdles. Denise got a big laugh out of that, but she found a few in my chest and gave them to her.

After my hysterectomy, I let myself go. Denise was it. Clarence and I wanted more children. I used to kid him about collecting cars. "I think they've become your children, Clarence," I told him once. "You may be right," he said. My favorite car was a 1937 Oakland. Why, you could play cards in the back seat. Before Denise was born, we had a regular schedule. We'd ride around the park and stop for a walk through the rose garden. On Saturdays we had a trip to the A & P and then back home to do chores. Sundays we'd drive to Edgemont to have dinner with the in-laws. My father-in-law was a card. He'd always ask Clarence it he kept the prisoners in line at the jail. Clarence was a policeman, and he always said, "I'm the man." Before Denise was even a gleam, my father-in-law would ask, "Putting on any weight yet, Earline?" Then he'd laugh and give Clarence a poke in the ribs. "Pay him no mind," Flossie would say. "Jim is such a cut-up." Those were good times.

> *They are not long, the days of wine and roses:*
> *Out of a misty dream*
> *Our path emerges for a while, then closes*
> *Within a dream.*

I always liked that verse.

I wonder what Chuckie will bring me from Wal-Mart's. He sometimes eats down there and brings me back a sandwich. Denise may bring us the special of the day. I never liked Wal-Mart. I was a K-Mart person. I liked to stroll through their food section, looking for tea and marmalade. I used to find them from Bewley's in Dublin. That's a tearoom my mother went to once and talked about forever. That was a long time ago before they came over.

When Sylvia and I got on my father's nerves, he'd lean back in his Morris chair, take out his pipe, and recite:

> *I will arise and go now, and go to Innisfree,*
> *And a small cabin build there, of clay and wattles made;*
> *Nine bean rows will I have there, a hive for the honey bee,*
> *And live alone in the bee-loud glade.*

When I was a teenager, I asked my father about their village and told him I wanted to see it.

"Don't go there," he said. You'll find some relatives, and they'll want money."

"Oh, Dad," I said. "They won't be like that."

"You don't know them. They'd steal coins off their grandmother's eyes."

"I'd never heard that. It must have been a saying. My mother used to say, "No rest for the wicked," but Denise says, "No rest for the weary," when she comes home from Wal-Mart.

Now my neighbor on the other side, Frances, told me she once went to Scotland and looked up an uncle. Her mother kept saying, "Oh, you must go see your Uncle Ian," so she and her husband and little Gloria took a train from Edinburgh to his village. They asked where he lived, and a passerby walked them to his cottage. He wasn't home, so they knocked up the neighbor. That's what they say over there. She said, "Oh, he's a regular down at The Old Woman." They walked down, and there he was in a corner crumpled up over a pint. He walked them back to the cottage. He lived alone, "a proper old bachelor" as neighbor said. He never offered them a cup of tea or anything else. "Why didn't you ask?" I said. Frances just shook her head. I would have asked him if he had a cuppa to spare just to see his reaction. Frances is not like that. It's a funny old world, isn't it? People want to get in touch with their roots, you know. Scott knew how to put it:

Breathes there the man, with soul so dead,
Who never to himself hath said,
This is mi' own, my native land?

I wonder what has happened to Chuckie. He's sometimes late. I don't tell Denise. He doesn't like to "granny-sit" as he calls looking after me. Maybe I should go out to that place with Sylvia. I don't have the money though. Clarence used it up with the nursing home. I've got the house, and that's about all.

I don't feel that I have the house anymore though. The living room and dining room are shut off. All those antiques we collected over the years looking like a seedy junk shop. I used to give parties, and then there were the Thanksgiving and Christmas dinners. Oh, well, what's the use?

Maybe Chuckie has gone to a movie. He likes those "blow 'em up" movies. I tell him that they are terrible. I can look at the ads on TV and know how bad they are— especially for young people.

Chuckie said to me, "They're great special effects. Grandma."

"But they're killing each other, Chuckie."

It's only movies, Grandma. They're not real."

"But they stay in your head anyway," I told him. That's what I worry about.

You know what stays in my head? Poetry and songs. Sometimes when I'm by myself, I'll just start singing or reciting. Here's one I like:

We are the music-makers
And we are the dreamers of dreams
Wandering by lone sea-breakers,
And sitting by desolate streams

I used to read to Denise and to Chuckie when they were little, but they don't remember anything. I used to sing and recite in school, but they don't do that anymore. Who cares? Imagine being my age and all you can remember is a violent movie and a cheeseburger.

Well, it's four o'clock. Chuckie probably forgot. I think I'll go to the drugstore. If I sit down a few times along the way, I can make it. Maybe I'll see someone to talk with. If not, I can always sing or recite and remember the good times when "God's in His heaven and all's right with the world." That's Browning, you know.

Higher Ground

As Betty Jean turns into the driveway, she knows that tonight will be just like all the nights of the last month after her mother Marnie came to live with them. She had been living in the North Georgia mountains in a small house she could no longer keep up, and as her only daughter Betty Jean felt that she had to take her in. Betty Jean's house was already full: she and her husband Big Billy, their daughter Sue, who works at a beauty shop, Little Billy, who never can decide what he wants to do, and during the day her granddaughter Michelle, who is their other son's child. Mamie's arrival has made things tight, but the upside is that Marnie looks after Michelle when she comes home from school.

Betty Jean gathers up her groceries and opens the door. Michelle is always waiting. "When's supper going to be ready, Grandma?"

"Here, Michelle, get a granola bar over in the cabinet and go watch TV. Did you get a coke when you came in?"

"There aren't any."

"I remember now. Your Aunt Sue drank the last one this morning for breakfast. I've told her a thousand times not to drink soft drinks for breakfast. I can't keep a thing in this house. If it's not Coke, it's Mountain Dew or Dr. Pepper. I can't find nothing she don't like." She continues working at the sink peeling potatoes. The chicken pieces are waiting next to a hot skillet. Betty Jean leans out of the breezeway door. "Mama, you can come fry up this chicken now. I'm going off to that country party Gloria is giving, and it starts at 7:30. Big Billy may be late, and I don't know when Little Billy will grace us with his presence."

Her mother comes in slowly from the carport, where she's been sitting. She had her eightieth birthday a few weeks ago, and she looks "as spry as a sparrow," according to her son-in-law. Sometimes she complains about the arthritis in her fingers, but she gets around enough to make beds and wash dishes, and do a little cooking. She's always waiting for Michelle to come home from third grade. All the family go out to work, and she likes to say that she keeps the home fires burning.

"Did you salt the chicken, Betty Jean?"

"We're trying to cut out salt, Mama. You can salt it on your plate." Her mother flours the chicken and eases it into the skillet.

"Is Debbie picking up Michelle tonight or is she leaving her here? She was supposed to call you at home. Did she?"

"I didn't get no calls today, Betty Jean."

"That's the tough thing about divorces—just deciding who's got the child and where are they going to drop her. I guess she'll come by for her."

The two women stand together near the stove. Betty Jean is taller than her mother and much larger. In the den she has an exercise cycle, which she sometimes pedals while she's watching TV. Her husband Billy tells her he has to take her to the gin house and weigh her and then have her mouth wired together for a few weeks. He calls his mother-in-law the little woman, and everyone laughs except for Betty Jean.

Betty Jean looks on the counter. "Was there any mail? I haven't had a minute to spare since I got home."

"I put it all over there on the TV except for a letter I got from Cousin Vonnie."

"Which one of your cousins is she, Mama?"

"Oh, you remember her. She's Uncle Homer's last girl— the only one left in the family now."

"What does she want?"

"She wants me to come up to Boone for a family reunion at Thanksgiving and stay with her for a while."

"Well, you can't go. Big Billy has his heart set on hunting, and I've go to work Friday and Saturday. I wouldn't trust Sue or Little Billy to take you. They'd be busy anyway."

"I guess it would be too much for me, but it sure would be good to see everybody up that way. I guess the last time I went up there was in the early 50's sometime when you were in high school. Your daddy took a notion to take us to the mountains for a vacation, and we all got together at church for a dinner on the ground."

"I remember, Mama. Seems a thousand years ago."

"I hate to write Cousin Vonnie though. She says that she's done the cleaning, and she's just waiting for me."

"After all these years I'm surprised she could find you."

"She got my address from some people she knew up near me."

The phone rings next to Michelle, whose attention never leaves the TV. The phone rings again.

"Michelle, turn down that TV and answer the phone. I can hardly hear myself think with this chicken frying and your granny talking." She continues making potato salad and stops to take tomatoes from the refrigerator.

Marnie turns the chicken and looks through the window to see who has come into the driveway. It's Sue in her Stingray, which she bought after she decided to live at home rather than take an apartment. "If you stay with us, Sue, you'll have more money for things you want," her mother had said.

"Grandmother," Michelle calls. "My mama wants to talk with you."

Betty Jean leaves the sink, tells her mother to finish the salad and goes to the phone.

"Sure, honey, that's all right. She can stay with us. There's always room on the couch for a stray child. I'll pick up her clothes when I go out. Just put them in a plastic bag in the carport. See you or Freddy tomorrow afternoon."

"Ain't she coming to get Michelle?" Her mother asks when she returns to the kitchen.

"No, she's got to go back to work tonight. She's taking someone's place. They're real busy now with computer work." Betty Jean continues working at the counter slicing tomatoes and glances over at the empty table. "Better set a place for Sue, Michelle.

Michelle doesn't seem to hear Betty Jean. She sits in front of the TV, and Betty Jean goes over to the washing machine and begins transferring clothes to the dryer.

"There's no rest for the weary. Seems like there's always something to be done. Little Billy said he didn't have no more clothes after today." She finishes, turns on the dryer, and yells at Michelle again.

The chicken is ready now. Her mother puts the platter on the table. The tomatoes and salad are there already. Betty Jean puts out a loaf of white bread and a stick of margarine.

Marnie begins pouring tea from two pitchers. "I made the iced tea this afternoon, Betty Jean. Both kinds. Sugar and NutraSweet. Yours is on the left."

"Thanks, Mama" She begins drinking tea. "Didn't Sue ever come into the house?"

"You missed her while you were on the phone. She's changing clothes."

"You know she's going out to a Barbara Mandrell concert with some of her friends from work. I ought to be going myself. I just love that little bit of a thing prancing around on stage. She's a favorite of Billy's, too."

Marnie lowers her voice. "Now don't Sue beat all? She works all day and stays out every night just like a lady of leisure. She and Little Billy have got their days and nights mixed up. They probably take naps on their jobs."

"Well, you're only young once, Mama, and they've got a lot of opportunities I never had."

The phone rings. Betty Jean gets up to answer it. "You'll get a sandwich later? That's o.k. We're having fried chicken, so I'll put some in the refrigerator for you. Now remember that I'm going to the country party tonight, so just Michelle and Mama will be here." She hangs up and looks at Michelle. "Will you wash up for supper, young lady? Now scoot."

Michelle slowly moves toward the bathroom. Betty Jean watches the TV for a few minutes and leaves it on. "Big Billy won't be with us, so just the four of us." She removes a place setting. She calls Sue and takes her place at the table.

Sue, dressed in tight jeans, boots, and a T-shirt that says "Get to Know Me," comes in, pivots one way and then another, and stretches out her hands. "Notice anything about me?"

"My Lord, Sue, what have you done to your nails?" Betty Jean asks.

"Got me some sculptured nails. What do you think?"

"You ought to have your head examined. How are you going to do shampoos with those things on?"

Her grandmother just stares at Sue's fingers and shakes her head.

"Oh, I can do most things - except maybe buttons and zippers."

Michelle comes in and takes Sue's hands. "I think they're real beautiful, Aunt Sue. I'm going to get me some one day."

"You just go sit down for some supper, Miss Michelle, and forget those fingernails," Betty Jean says.

"Aw, grandma. Not iced tea. I want a soft drink. Mama always lets me have soft drinks with my supper."

"Well, you're not at home now, and you can have iced tea. Besides, I'm out of drinks. Your Aunt Sue here has a steady diet of them. You want to eat with us, Sue. We set you a place."

"I told you I'd grab a bite with the crowd. I'm off right now. Goodbye, everybody."

"You drive careful, Sue. You don't want to put that Stingray in your daddy's shop."

"Oh, Mama."

She leaves, and Betty Jean turns to Michelle. "You say the blessing, Michelle."

"For these and all our many blessings we give thanks. Amen."

"Thank you, Michelle."

They pass the food and begin eating. There are three of them at the big table. Little Billy usually gets home too late for a meal with the family, and he eats leftovers.

"You know, Betty Jean, I bet a lot has changed up in the mountains since we were there."

"You know it. I hear there's condos going up every-which-a-way. A friend says they look like stacked trailers. It's them Floridians that want those new places. They're so used to them in Florida they can't hardly exist without them wherever they go."

"At least in my old place there weren't no condos."

"Grandma, I've got to take in some brownies for school tomorrow. We're giving Miss Hall a birthday party."

"Did you tell your mother, Michelle?"

"I did, but I know she forgot."

"I'm going out tonight, and I don't want to cook brownies before breakfast." Betty Jean continues eating and looks at her mother.

"I guess Michelle and I could follow a mix together, couldn't we?"

"Could we, Grandma Marnie?"

Betty Jean gets up. "Let me check and see if I have a mix." She goes over to the cabinet, pulls out a box, and returns to the table. She looks at the food, but she doesn't eat.

"You're not eating much, Betty Jean."

"I'm not hungry now, and I know Gloria will have some kind of big dessert from Southern Living. She always does. No wonder I'm overweight." She pushes away her uneaten food and finishes her tea and leaves the room.

"We'll have to do the dishes now, Michelle. You clear the table, and I'll fix the water."

Betty Jean comes back to the door. "Mama, I forgot. Gloria wanted me to ask you if you'd like to show that quilt at the party tonight. She thinks she might be able to get $300 for it."

"I don't know. I thought maybe somebody in the family would like it."

"They don't have no interest, Mama. They'll pick up some comforter over there at the outlet store if they need one. If Sue gets married, she's been talking about some satin bedroom set in a catalogue."

"Three hundred dollars is a right smart of money, ain't it? I guess it will be all right to sell it." She continues her work, and Michelle begins drying. Betty Jean goes back to the bedroom to dress.

"Do you have any homework tonight?"

"We don't hardly ever have homework, Grandma Marnie. Third grade is easy."

Marnie looks at her carefully and wonders whether third grade is that easy. Betty Jean says that Michelle has learned next to nothing in three years of school. They finish the dishes, and Michelle looks for a pan for the brownies. They mix the ingredients and put the pan in the oven.

Betty Jean comes through with the quilt. It's the Dresden plate pattern in pinks and greens. "Well, we'll see how country these folks are tonight, Mama."

"Okay. Have a good time."

Michelle is now back in front of the TV. The timer is set for the brownies, and Marnie comes into the den, her letter in her hand. She sits down and reads part of it again. She knows that she would really enjoy this visit. Talking about the old days is always interesting to her. She looks at Michelle, now involved with Family Feud, and knows that her great-granddaughter will never have such memories. She begins to think that if the quilt sells she'll take the money and go home. That word sounds funny after all these years, but she knows that home for her will always be her childhood home in the Blue Ridge mountains. Her childhood home, that's what she wants to see. It's too flat here to be her home; the air is too still.

By the time Betty Jean comes in, her mother has long been in bed. Michelle is asleep in the living room, and Big Billy is watching the news. From the bedroom, Marnie can hear them talking, but the TV drowns out the words. She has been reading The Upper Room, but now she is about to drift off. She does not like this room. She does not like this house. "There's no air to breathe," she says. She always wants to open windows. On the farm, windows were always open in her bedroom. The last thing that Harlan used to do at night was open the window. Now going to sleep is always difficult in this tight little room.

Several hours later she comes awake suddenly. She thinks she is dying. She turns on the light and the digital clock says 1:23. She goes to the window for air, but she forgets that the windows are painted shut. She kneels down on the carpet and begins to think of mountain air. She thinks of open-air revivals, where they sang the old hymns. The words of one come to her as a prayer: "Lord, plant my feet on higher ground." She goes back to bed and reads a little more and turns out the light.

In the morning she tries to stay in bed so that everyone can leave, but she has too long been an early riser. When she opens her door, she sees the door open to the den. Sometimes Little Billy falls asleep in front of the late show and sleeps all night in the Barcalounger. They are all in the kitchen now. She ties up her robe and wanders in.

"Well, Miss Marnie, you got a big day planned?" This is Big Billy's question every morning. He is a big man, hardly recognizable as a former high school quarterback. He takes pills for high blood pressure and wears a cap to cover his baldness. Betty Jean always reminds him to take it off at the table. He is standing in front of the television news, a cup of coffee in his hand. Betty Jean is frying bacon.

Marnie shakes her head at him and gets a cup of coffee. "Not much different about today, I reckon. Just the usual."

"Not today, Mama," Betty Jean says. "I sold your quilt. Gloria will come by this morning with the money. She has to go to the bank first."

"That's good. I'm glad someone likes the quilt. That was always a popular pattern when I was a girl."

"Grandma Marnie, will you wrap up my brownies?" Michelle is standing by the table, ready for school.

"Sure, baby, let me get a spatula and a box." She stands next to Betty Jean, who is making lunches for the men. Little Billy sits at the table, half-awake, drinking coffee. At twenty-three, he still looks young

146

enough to be in high school. Sue is drinking a glass of orange juice. The back of her dress is unzipped.

Betty Jean sets out the lunches on the table. "Don't forget these lunches now, and you eat them." She starts toward the bedroom and stops to zip up Sue's dress. "You're going to be in a pretty pickle if you don't have someone to help you dress, Miss Sue."

"But I always do, don't I?" She giggles and moves toward the door.

Little Billy hits her bottom with his lunchbox. "Hope you chip them nails, Sue. Serve you right."

"When you going to start shaving, Little Billy?" Sue rubs his cheek, and he hits her again.

They leave and then their parents and Michelle. The television weather comes on, and Marnie looks at western Virginia. Clear and 42 Fahrenheit. She changes her clothes and begins the work. First, she does the dishes. Then she makes the beds and comes back to dry mop the kitchen and den. She looks through the sliding doors and decides to go out. She puts on Harlan's old navy cardigan, which she has taken for herself since he died. She walks into the yard. A few leaves have drifted from the neighbor's tree. Big Billy works to keep his lawn clean, and he complains about the tree. She once mentioned having an herb garden near the kitchen, but he said it would ruin his lawn. She looks from one house to another and sees cemetery plots around them. She is not ready to die yet. She finds a sunny spot in the carport and drags over a lawn chair and sits.

In a few minutes Gloria pulls up into the driveway and gets out. "Don't they give you a key, Miss Marnie?" Betty Jean has told her that her mother embarrasses her by sitting outside. "Why do I work so hard to have my mama sitting outside like a field hand waiting to be paid?" she asks. Gloria has no answer.

"I just need some air, seems like. These brick houses are so tight and still like so many tombs."

They talk about the quilt. Gloria has decided to give it to her daughter for Christmas. "She's been wanting me to make her one, but I know I could never make one as pretty as this one."

"Thank you, Gloria. I hope she'll like it."

Gloria gives her the $300 in cash. "Now you do something you want to do with this. Don't give it to your family. This is for you."

"Thank you so much, Gloria. I've got something special I want to do with it."

After Gloria leaves, she takes the money inside and counts it out. The bills feel good in her hands. She thinks back to the egg money she used to make on the farm. "This money is just for you," Harlan would say, but she'd save it for little extras for the family. This money is that little extra for me now, she thinks.

After she calls the bus station, she begins to pack a little bag and then decides to take more. Today is the day to go, she thinks, because Michelle has scouts after school.

If she doesn't go today, she'll never go. She knows that. Carefully she writes a note for Betty Jean and puts it on the kitchen table.

When the cab driver knocks on the door, she is ready. He takes her bags, and she settles herself in the back seat. She checks her bag for the money, and, satisfied, she pulls down the window and looks at the house. Just another box without any air, she thinks.

"Where to?"

"Higher ground."

"Ma'am?"

"The Greyhound Bus Station, please."

Held Over by Popular Demand

The door to the kitchen is locked. Shirley knocks. Her mother comes to the door after a long wait. She opens the door.

"What are you doing home?"

"I got a ride."

"I told your father to pick you up tomorrow. Who brought you home?"

"Jim brought me. He lives in Ashburn. I'm on his way."

"I told you I didn't want you to see him."

"Oh, mother. Let's not go over that again."

She takes her luggage to her room and comes back.

"What can I do to help you with dinner?

"You? You don't know how to cook?"

"Whose fault is that? You know I've asked you for a long time to let me cook. We don't even have any cookbooks."

Why do we need cookbooks? I know how to cook what we eat."

"Maybe we could try something different."

"Your father is satisfied."

"Is there anything else I can help with?"

"Nothing I can think of."

"At least I can set the table. When is Daddy coming home for dinner?"

"He gets off at twelve, and he'll be here in a few minutes."

Shirley gets out the dishes and sets the table. Her mother is taking up chicken from the skillet. Shirley takes tomatoes, squash, and cornbread to the table.

A car pulls up, and her father gets out. Shirley goes out to meet him at the door. It's locked. He opens it with his key.

"Why do you keep the door locked, Mother? It's not as if we live in a high crime area."

"You never know what's coming."

Her father comes in, looking surprised to see Shirley.

"Your mother told me to go to the college tomorrow."

"That is what Shirley told me," her mother says. That boy Jim brought her home."

"He's a nice boy to do that," her father says.

"Dinner's ready," her mother says.

"Let me wash my hands," he says.

Shirley and her mother take their seats. Her father sits down and says the blessing. They begin passing around the food. It's standard fare in the summer. Her father looks over at Shirley and smiles. "It's good to have you home a day early. How's college going? What have you been doing besides classes?"

"The big thing is my lead in the play, The Chalk Garden. I just found out that Deborah Kerr had the leading role in the movie. I had the same role. What a challenge."

Her mother interrupts. "You were in a play? I didn't realize you had talent for acting."

"All the time, Mother, all the time."

Her mother looks at Shirley and then says, "You know I told you to spend your time on your music. Just remember that's what I've paid for all these years—not acting."

Her father interrupts. "I think we should support Shirley in her decisions."

There is silence as they eat their meal. Her mother glares at Shirley.

"I'm the one to make decisions around here. Not your father. Not you."

He looks at her and then at Shirley, who is looking at her plate. He changes the subject. "You know, Irene, Marjorie is in town for a few days. I don't see my sister very often, and she doesn't come often from Jacksonville. I thought we could invite her for a meal. It won't be much trouble for you with Shirley here."

He turns to Shirley, who says, "I'd be happy to help out. I have seen Aunt Marjorie in a long time."

Her mother frowns. "I don't want her here. She is uneducated like the rest of your family. The last time I saw her, she talked about deer in her backyard. Didn't she finish grammar school?"

"Irene, you know that she has a nursing degree." Her father stops and waits for Iren's response.

"So you say, but I don't believe it."

"What do you mean you don't believe it?"

"People like your family tell lies, you know. Not like my family, who had important professions. They were admired in the community. My grandfather was a lawyer. My uncle was superintendent of schools. My aunt was a music professor at Bessie Lift."

Shirley looks from one to the other. She has heard this argument for years, and she always wonders why her mother married her father if she felt this way about his family. Her mother looked down on her father's family. They were not plantation people—just farmers." Every time Shirley heard the word deer she thought of her mother and Aunt Marjorie.

Shirley had her own word that brought back memories of her cousin Diane. During WWII Diane's father was serving in the Pacific, and her mother married someone else. Shirley was always compared to Diane by her mother, who would say that Diane had such lovely blond curls, not like Shirley's dark straight hair. One day her mother said, "I wish I could adopt Diane." Shirley would never forget the comparison when she heard the word adopt.

Her father looks at her mother. "Will you never let that go, Irene? I'm tired of hearing it."

He gets up from the table. Shirley thinks he's going back to work, but instead he goes to the wall cabinet. He pulls out her Lugar and puts it to his head.

Shirley screams. "No. No." She runs to her father and wrestles the gun from him.

Her mother runs toward the back door. She screams, "Come with me Shirley. Let him do it.   She runs into the back yard, still calling her.

Shirley is frozen, the gun in her hand. Her father runs out the door, gets in the car and leaves. Shirley wonders if her mother ran into the woods. She often wanders in the woods. Shirley looks toward the door and realizes that she has grown up in a madhouse.

She puts the Lugar back in the cabinet and begins to clear the table and wonders how long the long intermission will last and whether there will be a last act.